Scottish Home and Health Department
Scottish Education Department

Crossing the Boundaries

New Directions in the Mental Health Services
for Children and Young People in Scotland

Report of a Working Group set up by the
Mental Disorder Programme Planning Group
of the Advisory Council on Social Work
and the Scottish Health Service
Planning Council

Edinburgh   Her Majesty's Stationery Office

H.M.S.O. 1

ISBN 0 11 492357 4

Note by Scottish Home and Health Department

"This Report of a Programme Planning Group set up by the Advisory Council on Social Work and the Scottish Health Service Planning Council is being published for the information of interested bodies and those concerned with the future planning of relevant services.

The Secretary of State has indicated in his foreword to the Report by the Scottish Health Service Planning Council on *Scottish Health Authorities Priorities for the Eighties** that he agrees with the Council's assessment of priorities which places services for the mentally ill in the highest category."

*Edinburgh, HMSO 1980

Chairman's Preface

This report is the work of a Group set up by the Mental Disorder Programme Planning Group. Our remit was to consider services contributing to the mental health of children and young people in Scotland. We were therefore concerned with the conditions which promote the healthy social and emotional development of children growing up within their families, schools and neighbourhoods, and with the part which statutory and voluntary services may play. The full group met 23 times between 1977 and 1982 and much work was also carried out by sub-groups.

Our focus made it necessary for us to take account of groups of people who would not normally regard themselves as engaged in the field of mental health. Without doubt the most important among these are the children's parents, relatives, friends and neighbours. In a report which inevitably devotes a great deal of space to the work of professionals, it should at the outset be acknowledged that it is those who are involved in the day to day lives of children who have the greatest influence on their healthy development. Furthermore, playgroup leaders, teachers, health visitors, general practitioners and many others involved with families in the community have a substantial mental health component in their work. We believe that a significant part of the time of those more commonly identified as mental health professionals should be available to people in the community whose activities have an impact on the well being of children, either directly or because they are associated with decisions about policies which may affect them.

Although a major concern of the report is prevention of psychological disturbance in young people, we do of course recognise that some will need more specialised help at certain stages in their lives and we have considered ways in which existing provision for this may be made more effective.

Our working group was composed of people who had in common a concern for children in Scotland but who were drawn from various professional backgrounds. Our discussions led us to recognise that an understanding of children, and therefore effective work with them, is enriched by sharing the perspectives of many different disciplines and that the problems with which a child may require help are rarely neatly divided between our current organisational packages of health, education and social work. Therefore, alongside an emphasis on the necessity of interaction between the community and specialist mental health professionals, the report lays stress on the importance of facilitating interprofessional co-operation. Basic to this is the removal of some present barriers created by mutual ignorance of the assumptions and administrative frameworks of other services. Our report may seem to some readers to be unduly simplistic in relation to areas of their own work; it was the experience of the Group that what may be obvious to one discipline is news to another.

We are of course aware that suggestions for improvement of services may not be welcome in the present climate of financial stringency. However, few of our recommendations have major financial implications and indeed we believe that the co-ordinated strategy we advocate would result in the best use of the resources that are available. Moreover, the promotion of healthy development in children must surely be regarded as a wise national investment.

Many people have contributed to this report. Earlier drafts were circulated widely to interested bodies and the working group is grateful to those who sent us their comments. An invaluable contribution to the report was made by each individual member of the working group; but I am particularly indebted to Miss Kerr and Dr Morton for their great help not only in drafting the report but also in editing it after the final meeting of the main group in the Spring of 1982. I wish to express my appreciation of the help received from our assessors and from Peter Taylor and Florence Cruickshanks of the Secretariat.

Elisabeth Mapstone
Chairman, Child and
Adolescent Mental Health Working Group
September 1982

Contents

Prologue: Robert, Danny, Alan, Sally and David

The aim of this report is to encourage, in families and in the community, the promotion of the mental health of children and young people, and, at the same time, to improve the availability, accessibility and quality of the mental health services for this age group. Of necessity, the report concerns itself with general issues and administrative matters, but the reader may find it helpful to have some picture of the kind of children we have had in mind. The following illustrations describe some of the more serious problems which arise. In no way do they do full justice to the variety of situations, or to the range of services, which are discussed in our report: nevertheless, they illustrate problems that commonly cause concern.

Robert, aged 12

Although it had been noted during his years at primary school that Robert was a rather timid child, who withdrew under stress rather than asserting himself, no particular concern existed until he transferred to his local secondary school.

Robert began to stay away from his new school after six weeks, and eventually the school called in the education welfare officer. As Robert continued to be absent, he was referred to the Reporter and then to a Children's Hearing. In turn, a social inquiry report and a psychiatric report were requested. Subsequent inquiries revealed that the transition to a secondary school had been difficult for Robert as he felt he now had several teachers to please and not simply one. His stress had been increased by the fact that many of his friends had gone to another secondary school. Although in his primary school he had been a hard-working pupil, his parents reported that he had now become rather withdrawn. Eventually they had thought that he was ill and they kept him away from school; it was some weeks before they realised that he was afraid to attend. They had then taken him to school themselves. On one occasion his form master had come to the house to accompany him to school: Robert's response had been to lock himself in the bathroom. Closer inspection revealed that his mother was supportive and sympathetic towards her child, but unwittingly handled him in a way that undermined his self-confidence.

At the Children's Hearing he promised faithfully to attend school. However, events have proved otherwise. Time passed and he was given school work to do at home. Negotiations have taken place between the school, the child guidance service, the social work department and the child psychiatry clinic. It is now evident that if Robert is to continue his education, a residential placement will be required. The choice available is a residential maladjusted school, a day maladjusted school, with or without a residential hostel, a psychiatric unit or a List D School. Whatever placement is finally recommended, the aim will be to return Robert to his local school and his home as soon as possible.

Danny, aged 15

Danny has been a source of concern to various authorities for many years.

He was an unwanted, unloved and unrewarding child, difficult to manage since his earliest years. He first came to the attention of the school authorities because of his attention-seeking behaviour, his restlessness and poor social relationships. His father had minimal involvement with the children and the marriage, unstable for many years, broke up when Danny was aged 8. Three years later his mother remarried and while his stepfather showed some concern, Danny never accepted his authority.

In terms of his intelligence, Danny's school performance had always been poor, and as he entered his teens, it deteriorated further. He began to stay out late, played truant from school, stole cars and had violent outbursts of temper. With increasing loss of parental control, a similar loss of teachers' control occurred in school so that eventually Danny was excluded. This resulted in total rejection by his parents and he was brought before a Children's Hearing and eventually placed in a List D School. Increasingly rejected and insecure, he began to mutilate himself by slashing his arms. He also made attempts to hang himself, and on one occasion was nearly successful. Although placed in three List D Schools, he was quickly excluded from each because of extreme difficulty in his care and management. No adolescent psychiatric unit had the facilities to manage him. An adult psychiatric unit to which he was subsequently admitted labelled him as psychopathic and therefore untreatable, and he was placed in Borstal, at the age of 15.

Because of the current lack of resources for such seriously deprived and disturbed youngsters who fall between existing education, social work and psychiatric services, youngsters such as Danny continue to be a source of serious concern.

Alan, aged 9

Alan had always been a moody boy, whose parents found him difficult to understand and at times rather resistant to what they regarded as ordinary discipline. They became especially concerned, and sought advice from the family doctor, when Alan was sent home from school one day by his head teacher for refusing to play in the school football team.

From his knowledge of the family, the general practitioner suspected that Alan's behaviour amounted to more that mere stubbornness, and asked for the help of the child psychiatric team. After some delay, Alan and his parents were seen at a hospital child psychiatry out-patient clinic. Following three clinic visits for assessment, during which Alan and his parents were seen by three members of the clinic team, it was considered that the child was quite severely depressed in spirits and that this was related to the style of child rearing which his parents had adopted.

It was decided to treat Alan's depression with an anti-depressant drug. It had however been noted that the boy had an overwhelming sense of guilt which was felt to arise from his being constantly nagged at by his parents and pressed to achieve at school, at games and in his general behaviour to a level far beyond his capabilities, and this made it imperative that the therapeutic measures were extended beyond simple anti-depressant treatment.

Accordingly, while Alan's depression rapidly responded to medication supervised by the child psychiatrist, his parents were taught how to manage him more realistically by the clinic social worker and clinical psychologist. The help of an educational psychologist, who knew the school, was enlisted to guide his teachers in their management of the child.

After about four months, Alan's adjustment at school had improved greatly. In particular, he had gained in confidence and had begun to develop a pride in his achievements. His parents reported that they felt happier with him than they had done for a number of years. This improvement was maintained at follow-up after a further year.

Sally, aged 8

Sally was referred to a child guidance clinic by the head teacher at her school. It was reported to the educational psychologist that Sally was disruptive in class, cheeky to teachers, and achieving poorly.

When a school-based behaviour modification programme did not produce the changes required to help Sally to settle and begin to learn more effectively, the educational psychologist asked the social worker, based in an area social work office, to visit the family to find out whether further light could be cast on Sally's difficulties.

It emerged that Sally's behaviour at home was unpredictable. Although for most of the time she was happy and well behaved, there were times when she seemed distant and unresponsive to her parents. Indeed, they felt that these occasions were becoming more frequent. As there seemed no untoward stress in the family which could be responsible for Sally's difficulties, the social worker and educational psychologist sought further help from the child psychiatric service through the family doctor.

In due course, after a period of in-patient observation, Sally was found to have a form of epilepsy. When this was treated her behaviour at home and at school improved greatly. However, as she had got rather behind with schoolwork, the educational psychologist who had originally seen her arranged for extra help to be provided for her at school, and after a year Sally's school attainments were on a par with other children in her class. The treatment of her epilepsy is now reviewed regularly by a paediatrician who is in regular touch with the child guidance service. The child psychiatric team no longer participate in Sally's treatment but are available for consultation if required.

David, aged 13

When David was 5 years old his parents separated and he had no further contact with his father. A year later his mother was admitted to a psychiatric hospital and David, who had already been attending a hospital department of child psychiatry, was admitted to its small residential unit where he remained for the next year. When he returned to his mother she had already been out of hospital for several months and was living with a man and his twin sons. Within two months in this new family and school setting David was found to be disruptive in class and had been discovered stealing from his teacher's handbag. He was referred to the Child Guidance Clinic but almost immediately afterwards was excluded from school on account of violent behaviour to younger children. The Education Department subsequently arranged for his admission to a residential school for children with behaviour difficulties.

He stayed in this school for two years during which his mother had a further period in hospital, parted company with the man with whom she had been living, and was finally given tenancy of a local authority house. David's behaviour in the residential school improved greatly and for some months after his return home there were no serious difficulties. His mother was however again readmitted to hospital for psychiatric treatment and arrangements had to be made for his care by the social work department. He went first to foster parents but then, because his behaviour became unacceptable to them, was transferred to a children's home from which he returned to his mother after a nine month stay.

Over the past two years David has been in four further residential establishments; first in another children's home because his mother went back yet again into hospital and the children's home where he was previously placed had no vacancy, then in a child psychiatric unit after a further episode of violent behaviour, and then, after an appearance before a Children's Hearing, which referred him for three weeks to a residential assessment centre, David was admitted to a secure unit in a List D School.

It was clear from his early childhood that David and his family would require help from mental health professionals and indeed these have been actively involved with the family over the past 13 years. However, David's needs have been perceived successively in terms of psychiatric treatment, special education, care away from home, assessment, and control and containment. Consequently provision has been made for him in turn by a health board, an education department, a health board again, a social work department and the managers of a List D School. These different organisations have each individually catered as best they can for this boy but overall, in conjunction with his family background, the result for him has been an ever-changing home and school evironment which will undoubtedly have had an adverse effect on his mental health.

1 Introduction

1.1 Although a number of reports have been published on particular aspects of the mental health services for children and adolescents, there has been no previous attempt by an official agency in the UK to produce a report encompassing the wide variety of services involved in this field, with particular emphasis on the relationships between these services and on the way in which they should interact with families and community services. This is a serious omission, which we hope our report will go some way towards repairing insofar as Scotland is concerned.

1.2 While increasing attention has rightly been given, in recent decades, to the physical health of children, their mental health and development has not attracted the same degree of concern. This is anomalous, since the major health problems now affecting children are not so much the acute illnesses as chronic conditions, including mental handicap, psychiatric disorder and ill-health arising from family stress or breakdown. In a recent WHO report[1] it was pointed out that:

'The mental health needs of children, who comprise a very large proportion of the population of the world, receive too little emphasis in programmes concerned with health and well-being. Knowledge about psycho-social development and about child mental health is only rarely applied, an omission that is particularly dangerous in times of rapid socio-economic and political change . . . The basic requirements for normal psychosocial development (in addition to an intact nervous system) includes a warm and accepting environment with stable parents or parent substitutes who are sensitive to the child's emotional needs and who provide appropriate conversational interchange and opportunities for play and consistent discipline, supervision and support. In addition, there must be the possibility of increasing autonomy and independence, adequate interaction with other children and adults outside the home, and suitable learning opportunities.'

1.3 It was this situation which prompted the Mental Disorder Programme Planning Group to set up the Child and Adolescent Mental Health Working Group in November 1977. The remit of the Working Group was "To review the mental health services for children and adolescents in Scotland and to make recommendations".

1.4 As far as this age group is concerned, it is essential to consider the promotion of mental health, and of normal development, as well as the specialist psychiatric services, and our focus has therefore been on mental health rather than mental illness. Prevention, indeed, however difficult it may be in practice, must be the underlying objective and, for this reason, we have given consideration to the more important social institutions, statutory and voluntary which effect the emotional health of children. This has involved us in looking at some aspects of education and of the administration of justice for juveniles. We have also given thought to the physical and social environment in which children grow up, since policies on housing, income maintenance and community development clearly have direct impact on their wellbeing.

1.5 The membership of our Working Group was drawn from various professions and organisations concerned with children and we have not always found it easy to develop a shared perspective. Those concerned with children and teenagers, however, always have much to learn about each other's work, and about the knowledge and values on which that work is based; and the effort involved in achieving inter-disciplinary cooperation within a common strategy will generally be rewarded. Indeed, in the process of preparing this report, we have become increasingly conscious of the fact that the maintenance of close relationships between the different workers, both professional and voluntary, in this field, and between the different agencies involved, is critical to the successful functioning of the child and adolescent mental health services. We have, therefore, laid great emphasis on developing a coordinated strategy for improving the mental health of children and adolescents. The failure to develop services in an inter-dependent way has resulted in disjointed and uneven development and, in consequence, the knowledge and skills which have accumulated in this field are not always optimally deployed. Moreover, not only are resources wasted when services are unco-ordinated, such lack of cohesion is harmful to children and their families. Indeed, it can be claimed that at present, structural and organisational progress in the mental health services for children and adolescents is every bit as important as further technical advances.

1.6 In arriving at our recommendations we have been acutely conscious of the constraints imposed by the current economic situation; but such a situation places a premium on co-ordination, and any initiatives which can be taken over the next decade to develop services for the mental health of children, adolescents and their families will be all the more effective for having been taken against the background of a coherent strategy.

1.7 We have tried, in this report, to avoid words which may have different meanings for different disciplines and terms, such as "mental health", "emotional health" and "psychosocial wellbeing", are used interchangeably. The varied terminology employed reflects the present concerns, perspectives and usages of a number of professions. The word "children" has been used, from time to time, to include young people. Our involvement with children's developmental needs is primarily, although not exclusively with their mental and emotional development.

1.8 The membership of the Working Group is shown at Appendix 1.

2 Developmental Problems and Psychosocial Disturbance in Childhood and Adolescence

2.1 No single approach is capable of encompassing the richness and complexity of the development of the mind in childhood and adolescence. Since misconceptions about mental illness and psychosocial disturbance in childhood and adolescence are still all too common, it is important to clarify the stance we have adopted on psychiatric disorder in this age group and to give some indication of the extent of this particular problem in Scotland.

2.2 Some mental distress in childhood is an unavoidable part of normal development. Young children, in particular, may suffer considerable anger and hurt as a result of frustration of their perceived needs; they may experience genuine anguish if they are separated from people and things to which they are attached early in their life; and disappointments, real or imaginary, can cause particular hurt in this age group. However, the intensity of a child's immediate suffering is not in itself a reliable indicator of long term harm. The degree of impairment of functioning in a child, as a result of psychological disturbance, may not be closely related to the severity of that disturbance.

2.3 Disturbance in children and adolescents must be assessed on the basis of judgements about normality and abnormality, and taking into account the presence or absence of impaired functioning. In arriving at such judgements, it is necessary to take into account the age, sex, life-circumstances and socio-cultural setting of the child, and the persistence, severity, frequency and type of symptoms and their relationship to different situations. In assessing the presence and significance of impairment of function, the extent to which a child suffers from his symptoms, the degree to which such symptoms impose social restriction, the extent to which they interfere with development and the effect which they have on others must all be considered.

Disturbances of childhood and adolescence

2.4 As the histories of Robert, Danny, Alan, Sally and David outlined at the start of this report show, disturbance in children and young people has complex origins which lie both in the child himself, and in the influences impinging on him. No clear-cut distinction can be made between mental illness and normal, transient disturbance of psychosocial development in childhood and adolescence. Psychiatric disorder in childhood and adolescence is an abnormality of behaviour, emotions or relationships which continues up to the time of assessment and is sufficiently marked and sufficiently prolonged to limit the child's functioning and/or to cause distress or disturbance in the family or community. We emphasise that the disturbances of childhood and adolescence, unlike most psychiatric disorders in adults, are much more specifically linked to development and must be seen in the context of the normal development of mental health in this age group. Furthermore, the presence of signs and symptoms of disorder in children and teenagers does not always carry the same significance as it does in adult life. Indeed, "many of the inhibitions, symptoms and anxieties of children are produced not by processes which are truly pathological but by the strains and stresses which are inherent in development itself."[2] It follows that children are vulnerable in different ways at different ages and at different stages of their development, and that the specific circumstances, or interventions, required to foster their mental health vary. It is also important to recognise that the majority of emotionally disturbed children can be treated by professionals other than psychiatrists.[3]

2.5 It is vitally important to be aware of the underlying factors behind a child's expressed symptoms. In general, these can be fully understood only in the context of the child's development and family circumstances—again, the examples we have given at the start of our report make this point explicitly. Robert's chronic lack of confidence in himself; Danny's inability to come to terms with authority; Alan's depression and withdrawal—these can be understood only in terms of the child's development and his reactions to it. Furthermore, a single type of "symptom" can carry different significance at different ages and in different situations. The temper tantrum for example, may be a normal outlet for unorganised psychological activity in young children, but it can also be an aggressive and destructive outburst towards the older child's immediate surroundings; or it can stem from an anxiety attack occurring, for example, in a child with sound personality development when he is exposed to psychological threat. These different situations must be managed in different ways.

2.6 Additional factors need to be taken into account in considering the emotional problems of adolescents. First, there are distinctive physical and psychological changes during this period of development, and important modifications also take place in the social environment of young people.

Secondly, a number of major psychiatric disorders of adult life can make their first appearance during adolescence. Thirdly, not all distrubance in adolescence arises for the first time at that age; a considerable proportion has its origins earlier. All these considerations point to a very wide range of disturbance occurring during the teenage years; and, in particular, normal adolescent development may itself colour the form which disturbance takes in a teenager.

Children and young people at risk

2.7 We are concerned, in this report, with the mental health of almost a third of the people of Scotland, ie those aged up to 19 years. In 1981, there were some 1,561,000 children and young people in this age group.[4] Current estimates[5] indicate that this number will have reduced to 1,352,000 in 1991.

Incidence of mental health problems among children and adolescents

2.8 There are no precise statistics relating to the incidence of mental health problems among children and adolescents. Survey of the general population in England, (we know of no comparable studies in Scotland), suggest that the prevalence of persistent and socially handicapping mental health problems among children aged 3-15 years is between 5% and 15% with a considerably higher prevalence in urban areas.[6][7][8] Three major groups of problems predominate, namely, emotional disorders, conduct disorders. and impairments or delays in normal development. A study carried out in the Isle of Wight[9] indicated that, amongst children aged 9-11 years, an estimated 6.8% suffered from psychiatric disorders of sufficient severity to handicap them considerably in everyday life. This should be regarded as a minimum estimate because the study in question referred to a relatively prosperous rural area without significant deprivation. In Scotland, a very different situation obtains. In their classic study of "disadvantaged" children[10] (a problem with which we deal in Chapter 3), Wedge and Prosser showed that, on the basis of a representative sample of children aged 11, one in 16 of the children in Great Britain as a whole would be considered socially disadvantaged. (The criteria adopted by Wedge and Prosser are discussed in paragraph 3.7.) The equivalent ratio in Scotland, one in 10, was the highest in any area of the whole country for which separate figures were provided.

3 Family, Neighbourhood and Community

3.1 Different aspects of the developing child's family and social environment may promote or hinder emotional growth and development.

3.2 The family is still the key setting for normal emotional, cognitive and psychosocial development; but family patterns are changing and we do not suggest that the appropriate environment can be provided only by the traditional nuclear family. We firmly believe however that, if children are to develop normally, their family, whatever form it may take, must satisfy, or be helped to satisfy, the basic requirements outlined in the passage from the WHO report which we have quoted in Para 1.2.

3.3 The child's developmental needs, including his needs for talk, play and exercising the imagination, have been summarised by Kellmer Pringle as love and affection, praise and recognition, responsibility and new experience.[11] These needs are, to a considerable and important extent, provided from within the family in its various forms by:

the provision of stable bonds or relationships which may serve as a basis for the child's growing circle of relationships:

the provision of models of behaviour for the child to follow by imitation or identification:

The establishment, by the adults of most significance to the child, of a set of attitudes which the child may follow or rebel against:

The provision of such life experiences as are necessary for the promotion and enrichment of development:

shaping the child's behaviour through selective encouragement and discouragement of particular actions, through the application of discipline, where necessary, and through the granting of freedom, where appropriate:

the provision of a secure base from which the child can test out new ways of exploring and responding to the environment.[7]

3.4 Like many other traditional institutions, the family is now undergoing changes from which its members are likely to emerge with roles which will differ substantially from those of two or three generations ago. Since young people are tending to move away from their original homes in search of better job opportunities, few young mothers and fathers now have the support of their parents, aunts and uncles and older siblings to the same extent as hitherto. Again, fewer women are confining themselves to a mothering role, and an increasing number of young mothers go out to work when their children are still quite young.

3.5 In looking at how families function, we have found it helpful to postulate a cycle of relationships between family members at different stages of development. Children, initially totally dependent on their parents, acquire increasing independence and then, in later life, parents may gradually become more dependent on their children. Normally the family accomplishes these changing relationships by and for itself without professional help or outside assistance, but sometimes problems may arise and, on occasion, a breakdown may occur, leading to the disintegration of the family or to serious difficulties for a particular member.

3.6 A stable, interdependent and complementary relationship between two parents—based on mutual trust—usually provides a sound underpinning for the satisfactory psychosocial growth and development of their children. Important aspects of this mutual support system are adequate communication, both within the family and with the outside world, and appropriate and effective ways of resolving conflict. Conflict may arise between the needs of normally developing children and the needs of their parents. In the long term, the ways in which these conflicts are dealt with can be as important as their immediate outcome, for it is the quality of relationships in a family which determines the degree of emotional security enjoyed by a child. Disturbances in the pattern of family relationships may be very subtle, and while they may not be at all apparent to the casual observer they may yet be injurious to the child. Inconsistent and contradictory expectations from a parent—or other adult, may lead to anxiety, over-conformity or withdrawal on the part of a child. The result is that his confidence is rapidly undermined and he may then take inappropriate steps to defend himself in a world which he perceives as increasingly hostile. The cumulative impact of inadequate emotional care, repeated unplanned separations from significant adults without adequate substitute care, and physical cruelty can be severely damaging to children. The witnessing of violence between parents, the involvement of children in adult sexual behaviour and their subjection arbitrarily to repeated oscillations between material indulgence and harsh ill-treatment may all be highly damaging. In such situations as these, children are at their most vulnerable.

3.7 Children may have considerable mental health problems despite prosperity: in particular, the demands on parents of a business or professional career can be damaging to children. Nevertheless, deprivation among low income groups is extensive and apparent. Stresses which occur in the life of all families are accentuated by such deprivation. Children disadvantaged in this way are particularly vulnerable in terms of health because of adverse social circumstances and poor environmental conditions.[10] Low income, as often as not associated with unemployment, inadequate housing, a large, or single-parent, family—these are all examples of factors which are positively correlated with retarded physical development, ill health and emotional disorders, difficulties of speech and hearing impairments, as well as above average rates of absence from school.[12]

3.8 There are, however, a number of "protective or ameliorating"[7] circumstances which can lessen the effect of some of these "at risk" factors and compensate for deficits in the experience of children and young people. These circumstances include good schooling, improved family circumstances and a satisfactory relationship with at least one parent and/or an adult outside the home (this being particularly the case in adolescence). Moreover, one isolated episode of stress is less damaging than multiple, or repeated, stress.

3.9 The inherent resources of the individual family are of basic importance and, the aim of services should be to reinforce the family's capacity to fulfil its essential functions, with the minimum of outside help.

3.10 Going beyond the family, it is important that the resources of the local community, particularly in areas of multiple disadvantage, should be mobilised to the fullest possible extent. Much hard work is needed to enable the community to develop and harness its own potential, and neighbourhoods should be closely involved in identifying—and helping to meet—their changing needs, with all that this implies in regard to community participation in the provision of the more formal statutory, or voluntary, services. Leadership, guidance and support from the professionals working in these statutory or voluntary services will sometimes be needed and an important and growing role of mental health professionals, acting with and through guidance teachers in schools, health visitors, educational social workers and volunteers is to serve as consultants to the community. This challenge must be accepted, because, where the members of the community are unable to express their needs and share in decision-making, the efforts of those working in the statutory or voluntary services can quickly become self-defeating.

3.11 In a growing number of instances in Scotland, initiatives of this kind have already been taken and neighbourhoods have been actively involved in working with statutory and voluntary organisations towards providing an environment conducive to child and family mental health. Where social action of this kind has taken place, the residents' awareness of the social and economic needs of their community—and of the effect of deficiencies on their personal and family life—has been sharpened. This has generated a desire for self-expression, kindled a greater social conscience and stimulated a determination to overcome health and related social problems. The establishment of community councils and local health councils has been a useful development.

3.12 In some areas of Scotland a system of working parties and project teams has developed, all formed from local residents and having good links with a wide network of statutory agencies. Such groups have been involved in aspects of community mental health and also in education, where, to supplement traditional school activities, resources have been drawn from the community.

3.13 We know of an example of community action which arose from parents talking to professionals who were prepared to listen to them, and from the professionals' consequent impression that such a service could add to these families' ability to continue caring for a handicapped member, providing a model of how individuals can work together in the community to supplement existing services.[13]

3.14 Some social work departments have also developed voluntary support groups, engaged in such activities as helping homeless families and families under stress, assisting people to adjust after spells in psychiatric hospitals or in prison, working in a new day unit for under-fives and visiting children in local residential homes.

3.15 There is scope for a greater range of voluntary work in child and adolescent mental health and there should be further study into ways in which it can be constructively used. In particular, there should be investigation into the possibilities of introducing voluntary help in the early years of primary school in relation to the behaviour and socialisation of children starting school.

3.16 In order to take full account of community initiatives, every effort should be made to involve non-statutory agencies, and the community itself, in the planning, management and delivery of services.

3.17 Effective prevention will often depend on changes in the broader cultural environment and in appropriate legislative support. In particular, we recommend that there should be specific educational policies directed towards increased public awareness of the needs of children and of the damage which can result from the ignoring or exploiting of these needs. Media pressures, particularly those exerted through advertising, can produce too early an assumption of "adult" values and activities among adolescents; and teenagers' expectations of clothes, records or cosmetics contrast sharply with the realities of unemployment and low socio-economic status. It is not surprising that, at the present time, many adolescents experience difficulty in coping with the divergent pressures of family, society and peer group.

3.18 We recommend that planning and housing policies should take full account of the effects of the physical environment on the mental health of children and that, in the development of fiscal and economic policies, much greater regard should be paid to the actual effect of these policies on child and family life.

4 The Mental Health Needs of Children and Young People

4.1 In general, the mental health needs of children are best met when all the relevant skills are brought together and are readily available to the community. The present multiplicity of services for children comprises one of the main weaknesses of these services. Children evoke strong, and often rivalrous, feelings among those concerned with their care and treatment, and this reinforces existing divisions in this field. The difficulties associated with the question of confidentiality are symptomatic of the resultant distrust among the professionals. Ways must be found whereby the various services concerned with the mental health of children and adolescents can increase their particular skills and at the same time, despite their different perceptions of the problems involved, develop their capacity to work together.

4.2 A positive interlinking of services, rather than mere co-operation between them, is essential. Their present organsation makes it difficult to deal with problems which cannot be neatly parcelled out to individual agencies. There must be broad agreement about objectives, and a coherent strategy, within which the different agencies and professionals involved can work together, and with the wider community, on common problems. This approach has important implications for organsation and training; we consider these further in Chapters 12 and 13.

4.3 If we are to foster the preventive approach which we consider to be paramount, altered patterns of work will be inevitable in other directions also. In particular, it will be necessary to increase the already substantial contribution made—in this field—by the primary health care team and other first-line agencies. If effective use is to be made of specialist staff and if the resources of the family and the community are to be properly developed, the general practitioner and the primary health care team have a key part to play in prevention, treatment and rehabilitation. (See Chapter 5.)

Parenting

4.4 Effective parenting is fundamental to the mental health of children and adolescents. As we have already pointed out, however, changes in values, in economic forces and, most important, in patterns of family living have altered traditional models of parenting and weakened traditional certainties of child rearing.

4.5 There is a growing need for information, advice and education about parenting which is aimed at developing self-confidence, an awareness of rights and responsibilities, an ability to cope and a capacity for relating to others. It is not simply a question of making advice and literature more widely available. Rather it is a matter of examining the factors which in practice promote the successful development of parenting skills. Parents' self-help groups, dealing primarily with practical problems, can help their members to develop self-confidence and awareness, and we commend recent experiments with parentcraft classes in schools; but increased health education in schools in planning for parenthood is a prime necessity. The report "Health Education in Schools"[14] recommended in 1974 that "each school should have a health education policy expressed in a comprehensive programme and should devise measures to enlist the help and support of parents". We recommend that this programme should include a substantial component on training for parenthood. The community education service could also have a role to play in this regard.

4.6 Readily available and easily accessible family planning services continue to be essential; and the advantages of family planning need to be more widely advocated by those involved in the other services concerned with the family and with child and adolescent mental health. Appropriate links between the family planning services and the mental health services should be fostered; and, where there is a risk, or a fear, of genetically determined conditions, both services should bear in mind the importance of offering referral to a genetic counselling service.

Mental Health Needs of each Age Range:

Birth

4.7 Childbirth is an important but normal experience; it is not an illness. Fortunately, practice in obstetrics is changing so that both the mother and the father are now able to give the newborn child a more natural welcome. The growing recognition of the importance of very early relationships with its parents has implications for maternity care which cannot be ignored. In particular, recent studies have demonstrated the significance, for both mother and child, of their first contacts with each other after delivery.[15] Attachment between parents and child, however is a lengthy process, with many other "milestones" after the first post-natal contacts; and care should be taken not to undermine parental confidence by implying that, because the condition of mother or baby was so critical as to require their separate care, or because the father was unavoidably absent, the bond between infant and parents will never develop. It is especially important that the care of mother and baby during and after delivery should be personal and sensitive, physical care being coupled with measures designed to establish the foundations of maternal confidence. We welcome the attention now being paid by the obstetric and midwifery professions to these considerations in their continuing review of practice and procedures in obstetrics.

4.8 Difficulties in the early processes of attachment can be observed in the first few weeks of life. The significance of these difficulties is not always appreciated, but, in some cases, the child psychiatric team could be helpful. Experiments in a London maternity hospital suggest that a developmental psychologist working permanently in the unit may be able to make a valuable contribution. The problems encountered in accepting, relating to, and handling a handicapped baby illustrate some of the difficulties which can arise at this stage:[16, 17] early counselling and support can often prevent rejection. Where problems have serious implications for the child's future emotional and social development, the child psychiatric team should be brought in, immediately, to work along with the primary care team. At this stage, as at other stages in the child's life, close liaison with adult psychiatry will sometimes be required.

4.9 A considerable number and range of professionals are involved in the neo-natal stage, and mental health needs may be lost sight of among so many interests. There is now a much broader range of classes in child rearing, parentcraft and "father involvement", all of which undoubtedly contribute to a better awareness of the mental health aspects of parenthood. Every opportunity should be taken, however, to improve the quality of these services, and resources should be available to allow parents who drop out to be followed up. The problem of drawing the line between caring and intruding, in this respect, has implications both for the professional training of those involved and for the evaluation of the services concerned.

4.10 Both primary care and specialist services are involved in identifying unwanted pregnancies, parental mental ill-health and intractable social problems. This is a particularly important aspect of their work because in recent years there have been major changes in social, cultural and legal attitudes towards, for example, single parenthood and teenage pregnancy, which have been shown by research to be associated with mental health problems in parent and child.[12]

4.11 Since there is no doubt that the quality of ante-natal, peri-natal and post-natal care given to mothers has an effect on the subsequent health of their children, we recommend that staff working in the maternity services should be made aware of the contribution that can be made by consultation with the child and family mental health services and, where acceptable and necessary, by their intervention. It is important that any such intervention should not be imposed on parents.

The pre-school years

4.12 The years before school entry are of paramount importance for a child's mental health, since the rate of growth is then greater than at any other stage of development. As young children are remarkably adaptable, services for children in their pre-school years offer considerable potential for promoting psychosocial growth and arresting, or compensating for, the cumulative effects of deprivation in its various forms. Health, social work and education agencies should therefore be involved as appropriate during the pre-school years. In early infancy, however, the mainstays of health care, along with the parents themselves, are (because of their skills in developmental assessment) the primary health care team, the local child health clinics and the community paediatric services. The health visitor is a key figure in health surveillance, health education and departmental screening; but her importance in relation to child and adolescent mental health is not yet sufficiently recognised. It is the health visitor, concerned as she is with all the members of the family, who can, in her visits to the home, provide guidance to parents during difficulties in the pre-school period, and detect areas of needs which may call for referral to other agencies. Clinical medical officers also have a significant contribution to make; and this needs to be more fully recognised. Good communications, and suitable arrangements for joint training, are essential for the effective operation of all these services.

4.13 Although mental health problems in infancy are not always recognised, disorders of sleep, appetite and elimination, failure to thrive or language delay may all have specific mental health implications. Unless their significance is fully appreciated, there is a risk that the management of these difficulties will be inadequate. Infant mental health is a little-explored field;

but, since the child may often be a barometer of the family's health, better ways of investigating problems in this area, and of involving parents in their resolution, should be explored as a matter of urgency.

4.14 Not all families use child health clinics or other pre-school health facilities. This may be because they are not readily accessible, but in many cases their uptake is determined by complex social factors. Until the first, compulsory, school health examination there is no requirement for all children to be medically examined. While we are not proposing a further statutory examination, we do stress the need for a more positive approach to early detection.[17] All pre-school provision should be as readily available, as accessible and as attractive as possible, and there should be a wider awareness of the fact that all services for pre-school children have a mental health component.

4.15 The place of "developmental screening" in the field of child mental health has yet to be established. "At risk" registers, used in other fields to aid early detection and reliable follow up, may have some value in the field of child mental health, but this needs to be clearly established by further research.

4.16 We considered voluntary provision for pre-school children, and the use, in some areas, of educational visitors to involve parents in pre-school programmes. The voluntary sector's biggest contribution is the playgroup movement; in 1981 there were almost 44,000 children attending playgroups.[18] Underlying this most welcome development is a growing conviction that the participation of parents, and of the community, is of fundamental importance.

4.17 At present, education authorities have only discretionary powers in regard to pre-school children. Although we appreciate that it would involve extending statutory procedures to cover all children from birth onwards, we recommend that these authorities should have a duty to make provision for children in their areas below the age of five found on assessment to have special educational needs.

4.18 Many child guidance services run pre-school programmes for children who, because of cognitive, behavioural, language or other difficulties, need more structured forms of preparation for school. These programmes aim to enlist the active involvement of parents and they are sometimes conducted jointly with schools and with social work and speech therapy departments. We recommend the further development of programmes of this kind.

4.19 In recent years increased attention has been paid to the potential of child minding as an addition to the range of resources available for family support. The number of registered child minders in Scotland has risen from 461, caring for 1,012 children in 1976, to 1,707, caring for 3,567 children in 1981.[18] We note with concern the widely held belief that there are many more unregistered than registered child minders.[19]

4.20 We were pleased to learn of particular developments in Strathclyde and Lothian Regions, which are designed to enhance the image and improve the calibre of child minders. Strathclyde Region encourages people to offer themselves as child minders, with a scheme which includes payment of public liability insurance, practical advice, access to toy libraries, and grants towards essential equipment and alterations required for safety. In 1974 Lothian Region introduced, as an alternative to group care for some children, a sponsored service of day carers employed by the Social Work Department. Day carers are provided free to parents, and are linked, for support and training, to nursery classes. Children can attend these centres, or nursery classes or playgroups as their needs for social contacts develop.

4.21 We recommend that child minding services should not be limited to the under-fives; many children, particularly from one parent families, can benefit from after-school care.

4.22 Day nurseries and nursery schools are beneficial towards children's mental health. A number of education and social work authorities have jointly funded the establishment of children's centres, combining both nursery education and full day care. Other authorities have seconded nursery teachers to work in day nurseries; and some day nurseries are developing into centres for a whole range of services for young children and their parents, with "drop in" facilities and organised classes for parents, as well as child minder support and training, mother and toddler groups, advice centres and health visitor and social work "surgeries". Parents should be involved in all day care establishments; and we recommend that the question of mandatory pre-school provision should be re-examined, in view not only of the low level of provision in this country as compared with other European countries, but also of the benefits to be gained, especially by the more vulnerable children.

4.23 It is not enough for local social work and education authorities, health boards, or voluntary agencies each to develop services for the under-fives in isolation. There must be increasing attention paid to methods of improving the co-ordination of these services, and of ensuring their responsiveness to the needs of the community. Only in this way can the maximum potential contribution of all concerned be realised. We were heartened to learn that, in some regions, co-ordinating groups have been established to study the present provision of pre-school services, and to suggest ways of promoting co-operation between them.

4.24 Services for young children should have the following objectives:
—to recognise the children's problems and meet their needs
—to refer on when appropriate for investigation and treatment.

The Education (Scotland) Act 1981 lays on education authorities the clear duty to disseminate in their areas information as to the importance of early discovery of special educational needs and as to the opportunity for assessment available under the further provisions of the Act. It also gives the authorities power to establish which pre-school children in their area have "pronounced, specific and complex special educational needs" and to propose measures to meet these needs. (For school age children, this power becomes a duty.)

4.25 The Act also provides for the appointment, by the education authority, of a specific named person for each child requiring specialised services, who would advise the family and otherwise help them in dealing with the different procedures and agencies. The health visitor has a central concern with family health and the function of the named person may often properly be assigned to her; but where the child is handicapped, the named person might more appropriately be the educational psychologist. The choice should not be made solely on grounds of occupation or designation. Parents should be encouraged to choose, from among the professionals known to them, someone in whom they have confidence and with whom they communicate easily. This extension of their remit would necessitate, for health visitors, extended and improved training in the field of child mental health; and a substantial increase in their number would also be essential. (We do not however see the health visitor normally undertaking the role of key worker as this is described in Chapter 11.)

The School years 5-16

4.26 When the child enters school, the school health services supplement the services of the primary care team, including the health visitor. Health surveillance is maintained by the use of routine statutory medical examinations. Teachers, too can bring health problems to the attention of the school nurse or doctor, who, in turn, can advise teachers on their significance. Since schools have the opportunity to influence the personal growth and development of children over a long period, training courses should be designed to enable teachers to make the fullest possible contribution to the mental health of children. Teachers should be closely involved in decisions about children with problems which are affecting their mental health or social and educational development.

4.27 During the school years, school doctors and nurses, as well as general practitioners, can identify mental health problems. Children can be referred to child guidance or to the appropriate psychiatric team. It is sometimes chance that determines which way the referral goes, and, to avoid duplication and omission and to ensure appropriate follow-up, much greater co-operation amongst the various people involved is called for. The most difficult decision is the one taken at the the initial investigation, since labelling can occur with distrubing ease, and the often fortuitous choice of agency of first contact may too readily determine future treatment. Much joint effort by the many professionals and agencies involved is necessary to ensure that facilities and services are matched to the particular needs of the child or young person concerned.

4.28 The variety of individual and family mental health problems encountered, in particular during the primary school age range, is so great that no one agency could deal with them on its own. New attitudes are required on the part of all concerned. Above all primary teachers should regard it as legitimate to focus on individual children, and to have greater consultative access to the child guidance psychologist. Teachers and psychologists must be available for case conferences in the school and clinic; and these conferences should be organised by the teachers themselves, inviting others as appropriate. The stages of assessment described in the Warnock Report[20] are consistent with what we have in mind, in that Warnock encourages teachers to mobilise and share their own skills and resources in assessment and to extend the circle of consultation as situations demand.

4.29 Families coping with a mentally handicapped child need special encouragement and support. This may be provided by social workers or by educational home visitors, these being teachers who visit parents and children at home to give more specific advice and guidance (for example to the parents of severely or profoundly handicapped pre-school children, on how to promote their social and cognitive development). Children who are educationally very advanced may also have problems of adjustment; and more provision needs to be made for such children. The National Association for Gifted Children is an organisation through which such children and their families may come together, share their problems and pursue special interests. The Association also functions as a pressure group, drawing the attention of the authorities and the community to the problems and needs of their children, as does the Scottish Society for the Mentally Handicapped.

4.30 The school is an important focus for services for children; and, since virtually all children over the age of five attend school, the multiplicity of statutory services should make more use of the opportunity for co-ordination which the school provides. We welcome the Warnock Committee's suggestion, now incorporated in the Education (Scotland) Act 1981, of a named person to provide a point of contact for the parents of every school child who has been discovered to have a disability, or who is showing signs of special needs or problems. (See para 4.25.) Good communications between the agencies involved are essential, and a reappraisal of the relevant procedures in schools is now required. We welcome the allocation of additional resources to less successful, or deprived, school children, particularly when the school they attend is in an area designated as being one of special need.

4.31 The idea of a school health team, working at and through the school in order to deal more effectively with the child's mental health needs, is not acceptable to all members of the educational profession. Some teachers consider that schools should meet educational needs only, and should not be involved in a wider, caring role. We believe, however, that schools should recognise the invaluable contribution which they are in a position to make to the mental health of children, and we recommend that an appropriate member of the teaching staff, and the educational psychologist, should be recognised as mental health workers in the school. Others, such as the school doctor, nurse, social worker and visiting psychiatrist, should partici-pate when occasion demands, along with members of the teaching staff. It is important that the services of these professionals should also be available to private schools.

4.32 All teachers have an important contribution to make to the mental health, and general wellbeing, of children; and in secondary schools, there should always be close links between guidance staff and form and subject teachers, many of whom already demonstrate a concern going well beyond their purely academic commitments. Our approach to these matters may be resisted by some, on the grounds that the provision of help to individual children who are having difficulties will divert scarce resources away from the needs of other children. This is an important issue, which needs to be kept under review. While children presenting problems in school clearly need individual attention, a balance must be struck and continuing guidance should be available for all children in the school.

4.33 There should be provision within schools for all children who for various reasons may be excluded, or who may exclude themselves, from normal classes. In some schools where pupils can no longer be contained within the mainstream of the school, special units have been set up. Pupils in such units spend most of their time with one teacher but, where possible, rejoin their class group for some subjects.[21] These "Pack" type units try to reintegrate the pupils to normal classes as soon as possible. There is an extension of this scheme in Glasgow, where the three secondary schools in the Drumchapel area have set up and manage a joint unit within the community. Each school provides a full-time teacher to staff the unit, and takes it in turn to provide the chairman of the management committee. Ideally, unit pupils return to their own school for some subjects, and specialist teachers from the three schools share in the work of the unit from time to time. The work of these units should be formally evaluated.

4.34 An alternative approach is favoured by some members of the teaching profession, and we know of at least one scheme where a permanent, school-based assessment panel has been set up. This panel has two permanent members, namely, the assistant head teacher (guidance), who acts as chairman, and the school psychologist. The other members are variable and comprise the parent(s), social workers, guidance staff and class teachers as necessary. The view taken by those who favour the assessment panel approach is that every effort should be made to give support, within the main school system, to children who are having difficulties, by promoting flexibility in timetables and by allowing partial withdrawal from the general timetable. According to this view, the "Pack" unit is not a solution to the problem, since the reintegration into the mainstream of the school of children who have been segregated into a special unit is rarely successful.[22]

4.35 The assessment panel approach commends itself to us, but it also needs to be evaluated. It is possible that what is called for is a combination of both approaches.

4.36 Different provision may be needed where children show evidence of emotional instability or psychological disturbance. Although the facilities of a child guidance centre would in some cases be adequate, other children may need admission to specialised day or residential schools. We consider residential schools further in Chapter 9; here we wish to emphasise the need for education authorities to provide day schools for maladjusted pupils of primary and secondary age ranges.

4.37 Teachers bear much of the day to day load of behavioural and inter-personal difficulties presented by school children. We recommend that all teacher training, both basic and in-service, should include a more substantial mental health component. Moreover, although schools undoubtedly have a most important influence on the behaviour, attitudes and attainments of children, it is insufficiently appreciated that some factors affecting the ability of schools to cope with pupils' difficulties (including learning difficulties) are outside the immediate control of teachers, and can subject them to con-siderable stress. The adverse effects of stress on teachers need to be further examined; and there is a strong case for the development of an occupational health service for teaching staff as a partial solution to this problem.

4.38 In schools, as elsewhere, cognisance needs to be taken of changing systems of values; one such changing system of interest concerns discipline and control. The current debate about the use of physical punishment in school is a reflection of existing tensions. While we welcome the phasing out of corporal punishment, we believe that the issue of control within schools should be considered in terms of the wider issues of control and responsi-bility in families and in the wider community.

4.39 We support the view that attention should be given to changes in the basic educational curriculum. As most teachers will recognise, there is a need to look beyond the merely cognitive or intellectual aspects of develop-ment, to the wider concept of personal or psychosocial growth. While we recognise the importance which many people attach to "examinable" subjects, a curriculum which is going to meet the needs of young people living in an increasingly complex society has to be concerned with a much wider range of matters. We believe that pupils should be prepared more fully for adult roles within families and as participants in their communities; it follows that teaching relevant to human relations and social skills, to an understanding of local democratic processes, and to some appreciation of significant current issues such as law and order and the conservation dilemma, should occupy an important place in the curriculum. We also believe that the changed balance between employment and leisure time implied by the impact of technological development and unemployment means that schools should offer an experience of success in creative pursuits whether cultural, sporting or related to social service, which pupils will be able to continue after they have left school.

4.40 In recommending a better balance for all pupils of academic, voca-tional, practical and social subjects, in order to prepare them for a full life in the community, we appreciate that there are those who would resist this extension of the curriculum on the ground that, even if extra resources could made available, it would be at the expense of the more traditional academic subjects. In our view, however, it is more a question of adapting the existing educational system to new needs than of rejecting the three Rs.

4.41 There are encouraging signs in this direction, which we welcome; but, of course, the problem lies not only in schools but also in tertiary education; universities and colleges, for example, demand, as a pre-requisite for entry, particular scholastic qualifications which have constricting effects on the curriculum.

4.42 Rigid "age breaks" in schooling can often pose problems. It is increasingly recognised that, unless there are sufficient preparations for change and close liaison between those involved at the different stages, transition at a particular age from one level of education to another can have an unhealthy effect on mental development. This recognition has led to closer co-operation between secondary schools and their feeder primaries; and in some areas detailed programmes have been worked out for primary to secondary transition. More recently, attention has been given to the pre-school stage, and parents of children about to start school have been involved, generally through a series of meetings in the school, in helping to prepare their children for school entry. For children who are coming to an end of their schooling, leavers' programmes have been instituted. We recommend further initiatives of this kind.

4.43 There is a considerable divergence of opinion as to the extent to which parents ought to be involved in schools. Though most schools are, to some degree, committed to involving parents, the constraints of timetables can limit the time available for this. Current experiments involve open access for parents to schools throughout the day, including the times when their children are in class, in order to allow them to take part in education. We are fully in favour of such experiments. The setting up of community education centres within existing buildings may help to settle some pupils and promote motivation. Their contribution should be carefully evaluated.

4.44 Formerly, the needs of the community, which were expected to be met by the schools, were relatively clear. Today, the relationship between school and community is confused, in spite of some attempt to break down the barriers between them. The development of communications between school and community is a matter of the highest priority, which warrants further investigation and assessment.

4.45 There have been two recent projects in Strathclyde which have involved different methods of linking schools with the parents and with the community. In Paisley, educational social workers were made available for consultation by teachers, to develop liaison machinery between the schools and the local social work departments, to undertake long-term work with individual pupils arising out of referral from the school, and, finally, and most important, to encourage the schools to work with children and their parents. Such workers can make it easier for parents to come to the schools, and they can help the parents to interpret information from teachers. This often needs considerable effort at first because the parents' reluctance may be associated with feelings of fear, guilt and anxiety in relation to the school. Once the parents have been brought into contact with the school, better mutual understanding can be created. In Govan, teachers have provided the link, changing their function from a purely educational and remedial one to that of a facilitator between the home and the school. These "link" teachers work with children referred by class teachers; they give particular attention to socially deprived children and their work includes visits to the home of the child so that the parents can support and extend the "in school" work. Attempts are now being made to encourage these parents also to take part in educational activities within the school.

4.46 Both of these projects were designed to involve the parents and other members of the local community. In this way it was hoped that they would increasingly undertake responsibility for many of the community activities, which would continue when the projects ended. Similarly, the school may serve as a focus for a particular community, as in Craigmillar, where the voluntary organisations have divided their area into eleven small areas, of which seven focus around their local schools.

4.47 We recommend further experiments designed to involve parents, not only by supporting the school's academic work, but also by participating in other activities within the school, and by extending the educational process into the home. This is particularly necessary in areas of deprivation, where difficult social conditions are associated with a way of life which is profoundly out of sympathy with the work of the school, and which engenders low educational expectations.

4.48 In areas of deprivation, liaison between the teacher and the social worker is particularly valuable. The teacher may be aware of the effect of the adverse factors, but unaware of the more positive aspects of the home circumstances. Similarly, the social worker's knowledge of a child can be limited if he focuses only on the family problem and does not see the child in school. Effective working relationships can best be achieved if the social worker has a base in the school and is part of an educational, as well as of a social work, team. We note the long and successful history of school-based social workers in Glasgow, and commend the policy of Strathclyde Regional Council's Education and Social Work Committees to extend this system throughout the region as and when social workers become available. We consider that further experiments and assessments should be encouraged in all parts of Scotland, so that the potential of educational social workers in schools may be properly appraised; and, in Chapter 14 of this report, we recommend accordingly.

4.49 It will be clear that we are not concerned simply with those educational processes designed to instil into children sufficient basic knowledge to enable them to make their way in the world; nor are we concerned simply with providing health and social work services to help with the existing difficulties of children and young people at school. We are concerned with a much wider concept of education, which would have the aim of helping children to mature both intellectually and emotionally, and to respond flexibly to an increasingly complex environment. We have mentioned some of the ways in which adaptation to this broader concept might be effected, but it should also be borne in mind that education, in the full sense of the word, must be based on learning through contact with life outside as well as in the school. We have already referred to the establishment of links between social workers, teachers and parents and to 'preparation for parent-hood' courses in secondary schools. Further examples of what we have in mind during the late school years vary from discussions between adolescents and representatives of local government, industry, etc, on employment and the problems of the young unemployed to the appointment of school liaison officers from the police force.

4.50 Adolescents have needs and problems which are distinguishable from those of children, on the one hand, and those of adults, on the other. At the end of their school years, they constitute a special group who are moving into a new social environment and taking the first tentative steps towards the more independent status of adulthood.

After School

4.51 The transition from school to work (whether or not gainful employment is involved) or to higher education is an important stage in the completion of adolescent development. We wish to emphasise the potentially serious impact of currently poor employment prospects, on the mental wellbeing of adolescents between the ages of 16 and 19. We commend the further development of statutory and voluntary schemes to help meet the needs of these young people. We also consider that further research is required into the impact of unemployment on the mental health of young persons in their late teens.

4.52 In this crucial transitional period, during which problems of identity and of integration into the larger social framework are uppermost, the provision of accommodation for single young people who are unable or unwilling to live with their own parents is a high priority need. There are a number of possible ways of providing the necessary range of accommodation, which involve local authorities, voluntary agencies and housing associations; it is important that provision should develop, not in parallel, as is generally the case at present, but in a co-ordinated way, so that gaps and duplications in the accommodation made available can, so far as possible, be eliminated. So far as possible ordinary housing accommodation should be made available so that hostels would be necessary only for those who were unable to live independently. Alternatives to hostels are supported flats/ bedsits which could be clustered or linked to other flats or which could simply be independent units with support normally being given on a visiting basis. In supported accommodation there should be emphasis on those life skills which young people must have if they are to lead independent lives in the community.

4.53 There have been other interesting ideas whereby young people have been able to buy their own flats under interest-free loan schemes; and one social service's department in England has arranged with the housing department for ten units of housing accommodation to be allocated to the social services department and sub-let to young people. If the young people prove satisfactory tenants they are granted tenancies in their own name and a further ten units of accommodation are allocated to the social services department. Other experiments have involved young people in care sharing accommodation with community service volunteers and university students. We are aware of a proposal whereby twenty or thirty flats, grouped in clusters of perhaps five units each, would be acquired, with a central day unit providing education and training for young people. We welcome experiments of this kind and we are particularly well disposed towards housing department and housing association schemes which enable the young single homeless and young people leaving care to live in mainstream housing accommodation. We are aware that problems can arise with regard to tenancy rights and sometimes there is a reluctance on the part of social work departments to become involved in property management. Given a measure of goodwill on all sides, these problems do not seem to us to be insuperable and we would hope that they could be resolved in a liberal, rather than in a restrictive, way.

4.54 We recommend that counselling services be made more easily available to adolescents. These services can help them in questions of sexual maturation as well as in regard to unemployment, delinquent behaviour or the abuse of drugs, alcohol and solvents. Such consultancy services, whether provided at home, at school, through the health or social work services or through voluntary groups, should be available in addition to the ordinary health education programmes.

4.55 Although we have considered all these issues relating to adolescents under separate headings, it is important to stress that, for an adolescent, health, educational, behavioural, social and employment problems are so interrelated that, only if communications between the statutory and voluntary services, and between these services and the parents, are maintained at a very high level, can the resultant complex situation be dealt with satisfactorily.

a. *"The study of children with special educational needs"*

This amendment of previous Acts reflects official acknowledgment of a change in thinking. The earlier wording requiring the study of "handicapped, backward and difficult children" categorised the children as others saw them. The revised wording is in line with the preference of psychologists for a wider interpretation of children's problems and needs, requiring assessment of the child and his total environment before providing an individualised prescription.

b. *"The giving of advice to parents and teachers as to appropriate methods of education for such children"*

The giving of advice following assessment as above may involve a lengthy period of follow-up with support and guidance.

c. *"In suitable cases, provision for the special educational needs of such children in child guidance clinics"*

Psychologists are in agreement with the recent SED[24] and Warnock Reports[25] and advise that children should be maintained, as far as possible, in their local schools. Accordingly, they seek to help harmonise community and school and to assist schools, firstly, to develop resources for dealing with a wide range of children, secondly, to identify children with problems at as early a stage as possible and thirdly, to manage these children in class, or in school-based units. The psychologist helps to identify children whose needs cannot be met in ordinary schools, and he will do the same for children in day, residential or special schools, or units. He may work directly with the child, or indirectly as consultant/adviser to parents, teachers and others. The range of work now undertaken in child guidance clinics with children, and in other units organised and administered by child guidance services, encompasses a great deal more than was usually understood by "special education" and is now appropriately reflected in the reference of the 1981 Act to "provision for special educational needs".

5   Services for Children and Young People

5.1 The statutory and voluntary services which are directly relevant to the personal developmental needs and mental health of children and young people have grown in a piecemeal fashion. It is now imperative that a more purposive approach to their development should be adopted.

General practitioner services

5.2 The provision of a good general practitioner service, based on the care of the family, is fundamental to the maintenance of mental health in children and adolescents. To this end we support the moves which have taken place over the last two decades to encourage group practice, and co-operation with other primary care workers, and to improve the training of new entrants to general practice. The compulsory vocational training programme, and the development of a higher qualification in general practice, are two such positive moves.

5.3 We also commend the increasing involvement of psychiatrists, psychologists, community psychiatric nurses, social workers and volunteers in primary care. The attachment of such professionals and others to, or their involvement with, the general practitioner services gives an extra dimension to the role of health centres.

5.4 In regard to the mental health of children and adolescents, the most important specific requirement is that the primary care team should develop a new emphasis on prevention, which goes beyond the current immunisation programme, and routine medical examination, to include the early identification, by the general practitioner, of situations in which the mental health of a child or a young person is at risk.

5.5 Our recommendations for general practice have significant educational and training implications. We deal with these in Chapter 13.

Child guidance services

5.6 Education authorities have a statutory duty under the Education (Scotland) Acts 1980 and 1981[23] to provide a child guidance service, with functions which include the following:

a.   *"The study of children with special educational needs"*

This amendment of previous Acts reflects official acknowledgment of a change in thinking. The earlier wording requiring the study of "handicapped, backward and difficult children" categorised the children as others saw them. The revised wording is in line with the preference of psychologists for a wider interpretation of children's problems and needs, requiring assessment of the child and his total environment before providing an individualised prescription.

b.   *"The giving of advice to parents and teachers as to appropriate methods of education for such children"*

The giving of advice following assessment as above may involve a lengthy period of follow-up with support and guidance.

c.   *"In suitable cases, provision for the special educational needs of such children in child guidance clinics"*

Psychologists are in agreement with the recent SED[24] and Warnock Reports[25] and advise that children should be maintained, as far as possible, in their local schools. Accordingly, they seek to help harmonise community and school and to assist schools, firstly, to develop resources for dealing with a wide range of children, secondly, to identify children with problems at as early a stage as possible and thirdly, to manage these children in class, or in school-based units. The psychologist helps to identify children whose needs cannot be met in ordinary schools, and he will do the same for children in day, residential or special schools, or units. He may work directly with the child, or indirectly as consultant/adviser to parents, teachers and others. The range of work now undertaken in child guidance clinics with children, and in other units organised and administered by child guidance services, encompasses a great deal more than was usually understood by "special education" and is now appropriately reflected in the reference of the 1981 Act to "provision for special educational needs".

d   *"The giving of advice to a local authority within the meaning of the Social Work (Scotland) Act 1968 regarding the assessment of the needs of any child . . ."*

This broadly defined function brings the expertise of the psychologist into discussions and decisions about children of all ages and in a variety of circumstances.

5.7 Child guidance had been provided in most areas for many years before it was made mandatory in the Education (Scotland) Act of 1969. The impetus given by this Act, the demands of educational and social changes and, not least, the pressure of new ideas generated within child guidance itself, led thereafter to more rapid expansion both in the amount and range of the services provided. The aim of educational psychologists is to facilitate the optimum development—intellectual, emotional and social—of children and young people from 0 to 19 years.

5.8 There have been continuing demands made of child guidance services to increase their existing commitments; at the same time they are offering advisory services in new fields such as fostering and adoption, children's homes, adult training centres, the education of profoundly mentally handicapped children, handicapped children in ordinary schools, new multi-disciplinary teams, and toy libraries. These new functions are substantially changing the role of educational psychologists both within the educational system and in the wider field of child care provision.

Social Work in Area Teams

5.9 Some local authority social workers are employed in teams which work with children and families in their own homes within a defined geographical area, and which provide a service to children's hearings. As a consequence of the duty imposed on local authorities by the Social Work (Scotland) Act 1968 to promote social welfare, they are concerned with material and financial circumstances as well as interpersonal relationships and may give advice about entitlement to welfare, arrange day care, negotiate with other social services on behalf of families and provide supportive services including counselling.

5.10 More specifically, the concerns of the area teams include the investigation of allegations of child abuse, contact with "at risk" families, and with the supervision at home of children who have appeared before a Hearing, whether because they have committed an offence, failed to attend school, had an offence committed against them, or lacked proper parental control. This activity on the part of social workers helps parents, at times of special stress or difficulty, to maintain a better material and social environment for their family, to protect vulnerable children, and to avert family breakdown with the consequent removal of children from their homes.

5.11 Where it is not possible for children to remain with their parents, community based social workers are involved in making arrangements for care in foster or adoptive homes, or in residential establishments. We consider these aspects of their work in Chapter 7.

5.12 The activities of area teams have obvious implications for the mental health of children and young people. It is important that the social workers involved are not only knowledgeable about the physical, social and intellectual development of children, but also skilled in working with children of all ages and their parents. They may however also be concerned with adults who are elderly, offenders, mentally or physically handicapped, or mentally or physically ill. Current pressure, in qualifying courses, to prepare students for work with this range of client groups makes it difficult for social workers to acquire sufficient knowledge about children and parents in their basic training. We see a clear need, therefore, for the further development of relevant post-qualification and in-service courses which would be designed for those moving to specialist, community based work with children.

Intermediate treatment

5.13 "Intermediate treatment", a term coined by the 1968 England and Wales White Paper "Children in Trouble"[26] comprises a variety of ways, usually initiated by social work departments, of helping children in difficulties. The White Paper urged local authorities to develop programmes to fill the gap between home supervision by a social worker and full-time residential care. As with "residential care" and "home supervision", the phrase "intermediate treatment" defines an area of work without describing it in any detail.

5.14 In Scotland, intermediate treatment has developed most notably at centres, with full-time specialist staff. The usual pattern is one of groups meeting regularly and focusing on members' individual problems and development in a social-educational context.[27]

5.15 From the young person's point of view, an intermediate treatment programme has several facets. It provides:

a. a place, and a group of people, with whom rejected youngsters can identify, and so find acceptance;

b. a programme which is interesting to such young people and which is capable of widening their horizons; and

c. a setting in which these young people can confront the problems which they are experiencing or creating, and in which they can be helped to work out more constructive and effective ways of coping.

5.16 There remains uncertainty about the exact role of intermediate treatment and perhaps an underlying attitude, in some sections of the community, of fear and hostility towards young people has ensured that its growth has been slow and piecemeal. However there are now in Scotland a number of diverse projects at various points on the continuum of care between supervision at home and residential care.

5.17 Intermediate care is potentially a very valuable addition to the range of services; but programmes must be carefully planned in consultation with other agencies, and they must be evaluated so that a balance is struck between innovation and proven effectiveness.

Voluntary organisations

5.18 A number of voluntary organisations provide valuable services in this field. Some are concerned mainly with the provision of residential care; others concentrate on mobilising community involvement whether through the use of volunteers or otherwise; still others provide specialist field social work services. At their best, voluntary bodies can be extremely innovative in the services which they provide. If the contribution of the voluntary sector is to remain valid and relevant, a continuing partnership between statutory and voluntary services is called for, with financial and other support from central and local government. It is particularly important that, in the mental health services for children and young people, this partnership should aim at preserving the flexibility and enhancing the inventiveness of the voluntary sector.

Specialist child and adolescent mental health teams

5.19 Where they exist, child and adolescent mental health services in Scotland are provided full-time, with specific arrangements for emergency work where necessary. Most child and adolescent mental health services, as recommended in the Court Report[3] are provided on a co-ordinated basis by interdisciplinary child and adolescent mental health teams, which operate, at present, from a hospital base. The social work component of these teams is now provided from outwith the National Health Service, and they have recently had to take account of the development of autonomous departments of clinical psychology. Hospital-based child and adolescent mental health teams do not formally include educational psychologists; in most cases, however, they have regular contact with the child guidance service. Similarly, they work closely with voluntary agencies.

5.20 For a variety of reasons, the provision of child and adolescent mental health services in Scotland is still extremely patchy, the limited numbers of medical, nursing and other staff now available being unevenly distributed throughout the country. Where services do exist, they are often not well sited in relation to the needs which they are called upon to meet; and, more often than not, they have to be content with unsatisfactory and, in some cases, totally inadequate accommodation.

5.21 Until recently, these services have been primarily engaged in the provision of a specialist diagnostic and treatment service. This role remains of great important and is now, indeed, being enhanced by the progressive introduction of more effective techniques. At the same time, developments in the field of child and adolescent mental health in recent years have led to increased demands on child and adolescent mental health professionals, particularly child and adolescent psychiatrists, to teach other professionals and to provide consultative services to these professionals and to the various agencies concerned with children who may have mental health problems. The more expert and, at the same time, the wider role, which these treatment advances and other developments imply, is entirely appropriate. In addition, as we recommend in paragraph 5.31, the child and adolescent mental health services must be extended to include the treatment and care of mentally handicapped children. Recommendations aimed at remedying these deficiences and stressing the need for all appointments of consultant child and adolescent psychiatrists to be accompanied by the appointment of other members of the specialist team, namely, nursing staff, social workers, clinical psychologists and supporting staff, are set out in Chapter 13.

Child and Adolescent Psychiatrists

5.22 The number of child and adolescent psychiatrists, in particular, who are available in Scotland, is inadequate to provide an effective diagnostic and treatment service, far less to develop this service, by taking account of more effective techniques and by providing wide-ranging consultation and teaching. We emphasise that the advisory, consultative and supportive role of child and adolescent psychiatrists is becoming more, rather than less, important.

Social Workers

5.23 The special importance of social work within child and adolescent mental health teams lies in its emphasis on understanding the family and social setting in which a child develops. It is this level and depth of understanding which enables social workers to mobilise resources of neighbourhood and community to help families; to ensure that the influence of social attitudes on child and family behaviour is given due attention in the planning of treatment programmes; and to make a contribution to such programmes where appropriate. If child and adolescent mental health teams are to function effectively, social workers within them must provide continuity of care and advice over long periods of time. This implies that such teams must maintain an involvement of social work at an appropriate seniority. We make further recommendations on this point in Chapter 13.

Clinical psychologists

5.24 The clinical psychologist contributes to the team a range of important functions in assessment and treatment. In most settings, his contribution comes through his membership of the multidisciplinary psychiatric team. We see the presence of a full-time senior grade clinical psychologist as the most effective way of providing psychological services within child and adolescent psychiatry. We recommend, therefore, that such a person be provided from the area division of clinical psychology or, where there is a specialist department of clinical child psychology, that a psychologist from this department should be attached to the child and adolescent psychiatric team. One of the functions of the clinical child psychologist so appointed would be to establish effective communications with the local authority's educational psychologist. There are many situations, commonly involving aspects of educational assessment, in which the psychiatric team requires the specialised expertise of the educational psychologist, as well as his detailed knowledge of educational provision. The arrangements for this co-operative activity vary considerably. In some cases, an educational psychologist is seconded part-time to the child and adolescent psychiatric service; in others, an individual educational psychologist, while remaining firmly within the child guidance service of the education authority, is recognised as having particular responsibility for liaison with these services. Such arrangements have worked extremely well to date and we recommend their extension to those areas where they are limited or have not yet been started. Similar arrangements should be developed between psychologists in the health service and those in education. We advocate the concept of child psychology as a specialty within generic clinical psychology.

Nurses

5.25 The development of child and adolescent psychiatric nursing has been seriously hampered by the lack of suitable post-registration training courses. The nurses' part in therapy in child and adolescent psychiatry is not always full recognised. In the development of the nursing services the emphasis should be on continuing care within the community. We recommend the provision of suitable post-registration courses and the creation of a sufficient number of specialist career grade posts to enable the development of greater nursing expertise in this area. These senior nursing officers should be able to participate in the interdisciplinary training programmes to which we refer in Chapter 13. We also recommend that health boards should examine their administrative nursing structure to ensure that expert nursing advice and support is available for the child and adolescent psychiatric services.

Speech therapists, physiotherapists, dietitians and occupational therapists

5.26 A number of other disciplines have a part to play in the work of the child and adolescent psychiatric team. Speech therapists, and, to a lesser extent, physiotherapists, and dietitians make contributions of great value. We are particularly concerned that the contribution of occupational therapists who wish to specialise in work with children should be recognised. In addition to assessing aspects of children's development, and their play, occupational therapists can contribute to a number of therapeutic programmes on an in-patient or out-patient basis. Although it is not possible at present to recommend specific staffing levels, we consider that the development of occupational therapy in the child and adolescent psychiatric service should be encouraged, and, in due course, there should be scope for an extension of the work of these therapists to day care centres and children's homes.

Team working

5.27 We have looked in some detail at the issues involved in providing mental health services for children and adolescents through co-ordinated interdisciplinary teams. Because the mental health professions have developed a range of highly skilled techniques of assessment and treatment, the team must, whatever its patterns of work, operate so as to allow all its members' skills to be used to the full. Awareness of the conflicts which are inherent in teamwork[28] is important: the aim must be so to develop a joint approach that such conflicts can be resolved by more sharing of skill and knowledge, by the growth of mutual respect among team members, and by leadership on particular issues being based on the appropriate ability and experience rather than on the profession of origin. Clearly the question of confidentiality arises, but an over-cautious attitude is to be avoided and great care must be taken to ensure that confidentiality operates in the interests of the children concerned, rather than as a protective device for professional staff. The greatest possible degree of participation on the part of the children concerned and their parents also provides an important safeguard where issues of confidentiality are involved. It is also important to remember that there is no inconsistency between real teamwork and a particular professional working with individual patients. In cases where the full team is not required, a decision to that effect should be made explicit.

5.28 Continuity of treatment, and adequate opportunity for inter-disciplinary training, depend upon the team's achievement of some degree of cohesion, through the regular working together of at least some of its members. It is only where there is a core, or nucleus, of committed profes-sionals that the team can develop, through its involvement with teachers, area social workers, general practitioners, paediatricians, health visitors, voluntary workers and others involved with the wellbeing of children.

5.29 So far as we have been able to ascertain, the different professions involved in the child and adolescent mental health services receive little or no formal training in teamwork. While those professions with a social science background may have a better theoretical preparation than others, it is far too readily assumed that teamwork is something which comes naturally, which can be done by anyone, and which does not require to be learned. All the professional and voluntary workers in the child and adolescent mental health services should have a significant element of their training specifically concerned with work in multidisciplinary teams and there can be no substitute for experiential learning in this field. We deal in more detail with this important matter in Chapter 13; but it may also be worth stressing, at this point in our report, that the successful working of the clinical team is dependent not only on individual efforts of the members of the team but also on the existence of genuine inter-agency collaboration between the different authorities involved. This is discussed in Chapter 12.

Specialist services for adolescents

5.30 We have referred throughout this chapter to joint services for children and adolescents with psychiatric disorder. In some parts of the country, services for adolescents already exist, but these are, to a considerable extent, separate from those provided for younger children, especially in the case of adolescent psychiatric services based on in-patient units. We recommend that in-patient provision for psychiatrically disturbed adoles-cents, to which we refer further in para 5.35, should be integrated with a comprehensive child and adolescent psychiatric service. The out-patient services provided for teenagers should be similarly integrated, although such integration need not necessarily imply provision of adolescent services in the same premises as are used for younger children.

Mental health services for mentally handicapped children

5.31 Mentally handicapped children and young people may have complicating psychiatric, or psychosocial, problems. A mental health service for children and adolescents should not make a distinction between those of normal intelligence and the mentally handicapped. At present the provision of services for psychiatrically disordered mentally handicapped children is haphazard; often they are looked after by specialists in mental handicap, some of whom, following the recommendations of the report "The Staffing of Mental Deficiency Hospitals"[29] have joint appointments in general psychiatry and mental handicap. Other children, generally those who do not have to live in hospital, come within the ambit of the child and adolescent psychiatric service. We agree with the report "A Better Life"[16] that, where the condition of a child in hospital requiring special in-patient services is predominantly physical, clinical responsibility should lie with the consultant paediatrician. Where the condition is predominantly a behaviour disorder, or other psychiatric state, responsibility should lie with a consultant in child and adolescent psychiatry or a child psychologist.

A new structure for the specialist services

5.32 Traditionally, the child and adolescent mental health service has had a medical base. We recommend that this should be broadened. Professional staff should be appointed to work with other professionals and to serve a particular area rather than be assigned to a particular professional task in a particular agency or institution. The functioning of the clinical team in the child and adolescent service could and should be safeguarded and improved by providing a structure enabling professions other than medicine, to contribute to the formulation of policy and the development of the service. Accordingly we recommend that the psychiatric, psychological, educational and social work components of the service should be united in a single child, adolescent and family development service with a division of each discipline within it. The attachment of each professional worker would then relate primarily to a combined service rather than to separate specialisms. While this sensible step would not require any change in the conditions of employ- ment of particular professionals, it would be of considerable benefit both to these professionals and, above all, to patients and their families. Apart from simplifying routine administration, it would make for the more effective ordering of priorities; and it would also ensure better arrangements for meeting teaching commitments and ensuring liaison with outside agencies.

5.33 We recommend that the proposed child, adolescent and family development service should be concerned with children of all levels of ability. It should provide an advisory and consultative service to agencies concerned with mentally handicapped children and, in particular, to the paediatric service. Clearly if the child, adolescent and family development service is to assume responsibility in this way for mentally handicapped children who need specialist attention, some redistribution of the resources being made available to services for children as a whole will be required.

Facilities required

5.34 Accommodation for the child, adolescent and family development service should comprise the following: a clinical and administrative base, an out-patient complex, an in-patient unit for children, an in-patient unit for adolescents, and a clinical teaching area. In some departments these basic requirements may be supplemented by a day patient unit. More specifically, each clinical team's accommodation should include office facilities for staff members; consulting rooms suitable for work with individual children, or groups of children, or families; a room for case conferences or teaching seminars; and accommodation for secretarial staff. Where younger children are attending, a playroom is necessary as well as comfortable waiting accommodation for parents and children. Full-time secretarial staff are key figures in departments of child and adolescent psychiatry and, as they undertake a wide range of administrative and organisational functions, we recommend that the senior member of each department's secretarial staff should be appointed at Higher Clerical Officer grade.

5.35 There are already psychiatric in-patient units for children and adolescents in some areas of Scotland. Their size and location varies; some are in the grounds of general or psychiatric hospitals, and some of those for pre-adolescents are part of children's hospitals. In 1981 there were 102 available staffed beds for children and 64 for adolescents. Bed occupancy, which in 1981 was 66.6% for children's beds and 72.9% for adolescents' has tended to decline in recent years, but it is not known to what extent this decline is the result of more effective treatment now employed in out-patient work, or is due to a shortage of nurses in in-patient units. We recommend that the situation should be kept under close review. In-patient treatment for pre-adolescent children should be provided in the ratio of 20 beds per 250,000 child population as recommended in the Court Report[3] with this target being adjusted as appropriate to take account of local conditions. In-patient provision for psychiatrically disturbed adolescents should be provided to serve each area, in the ratio of 18 beds per 250,000 child population, again with adjustment as appropriate to take account of local variation in need. It is acknowledged that very small units, whether for pre-adolescents or adolescents, will be difficult to staff. We refer to provision for adolescents presenting with particularly severe problems in Chapter 10.

Training and research functions of child and adolescent mental health services

5.36 Two important elements of the work of the child and adolescent mental health services are teaching and research. These are further discussed in Chapters 13 and 14.

5.37 Given the growing need to extend teaching and research because of existing pressures, and given, too, the immense importance of both of these functions for the future development of the child and adolescent mental health service, we recommend that, as soon as resources permit, Departments of Child and Adolescent Mental Health, closely associated with existing Departments of Child Health, should be established in the three Scottish Medical Schools which are at present without such Departments.

6   Children's Hearings

6.1 The children's hearing system illustrates the effort which has been made, through recent social policy in Scotland, to involve local communities in providing for children in trouble or difficulty. The panel members are charged, as ordinary citizens, with the statutory duty of making decisions about the compulsory measures of care which are appropriate to the needs of children, from their respective local communities, who have been referred to the Reporter. Panel members are chosen for their personal qualities and abilities, and should also represent the community's articulate voice and informed opinion. They have an important part to play in decision making; they are able to exert pressure for resources; and they are knowledgeable observers of the work of the various professionals in the children's hearing system.

6.2 In this chapter we consider, first, the response of the community, through the hearing system, when a child's behaviour becomes unacceptable or when he is deemed to be at risk of injury or abuse in his own home, and, secondly, the impact of this response on the mental health of children. A child appearing before a hearing is in a vulnerable position; and, since he cannot fight for himself, the hearing system must ensure that his rights are protected. The positive approach embodied in the concept of children's hearings is potentially more sensitive and appropriate than traditional procedures, seeking, as it does, to match the provision of care to the individual needs of the child in trouble or difficulty.

6.3 Most parents accept social intervention in the lives of children and adolescents in the form of health and education services. Generally, children and their parents are willing to cooperate in routine medical examinations, and to seek medical help in illness. Again, most people accept, within broad limits, the existing system of compulsory education. There are, however, circumstances in which formal state intervention may be both justifiable and necessary in the child's interests when the parents are unwilling to cooperate in his care or control, or are unable to do so without assistance.

6.4 The importance of taking into account children's own wishes when legal decisions of consequence are being taken about them has been increasingly recognised in recent child care legislation. It is all too easy to waive liberal principles with regard to children who are too young to understand the legal and social ramifications of their situation. Yet these children and, indeed, all children deemed to be in need of compulsory measures of care, have basic rights which cannot be ignored, including the right to adequate parenting, education, medical treatment and legal or other representation. The criminal law has continued to recognise the difference between child and adult offenders in the matter of culpability; and an appreciation of the extent of deprivation in our society must temper a too-retributive policy towards most of the children in our juvenile justice system. Nevertheless, children have responsibilities as well as rights; and it is not in the best interests of any child that his unacceptable behaviour should be excused or ignored, on the grounds that circumstances beyond his control caused his social deviation. Most children are willing to admit responsibility in whole, or in part, when they have committed offences, and most, in fact, feel the need to make amends. Sensible and voluntary reparation, as a means of assuaging guilt and discharging, at least in part, his responsibility to the injured party, is a desirable consideration in determining what is in the best interests of the child.

6.5 One constructive feature of the children's hearing system is its focus on the individual needs of the child. Another positive feature is the possibility which the system affords of developing for the child a flexible programme of care to suit his needs. Thanks to the safeguard of the statutory procedure. whereby all children subject to compulsory measures of care must have their supervision requirements reviewed within a year (earlier if the parents so wish), a child is unlikely to be lost sight of in the system. Although the emphasis at hearings is on the needs of the child, his parents play a significant part in the proceedings. Much of the success of the system depends on the quality of the discussions at hearings, and on the degree to which parents can be helped to accept and discharge their responsibilities towards their children.

6.6 Difficult and painful decisions are taken daily at children's hearings. Necessary discussions, involving highly personal matters in which both children and parents are encouraged to participate, take place in a way which would not be possible in the atmosphere of a court. A realistic attempt is made to recognise the true nature of the problem, in terms both of personal relationships and of personal responsibility, against the background of the community's interest in rectifying matters with the agreement of the parties present at the hearing. Notwithstanding the informality of the proceedings, which can promote discussion with him about the real issues which are causing trouble or difficulty, the child's rights are carefully safeguarded; and no discussion can begin unless the child and his parents first accept the grounds of the referral. Where they dispute the facts, the case either goes to the sheriff for proof or is dismissed. Where there is a referral in respect of a child who is too young to understand, here, too, the evidence must be laid before the sheriff, who has to be satisfied, in the interest of the child, that the alleged grounds for the referral have been established.

6.7 Every decision made by a children's hearing involving the imposition of compulsory supervision may be challenged by the child and/or his parents by appeal to the sheriff. Moreover, the child and his parent have the right to bring a representative of their choice to a hearing to help express a particular viewpoint and to give support throughout the proceedings. Section 66 of the Children Act 1975, which has not yet been implemented, enables a chairman of a hearing, or a sheriff, to appoint an independent Curator, or children's representative, to act for a child where there is a conflict of interest between the child and his parents. We recommend the early implementation of this section. We consider that further thought must be given to the selection and preparation of this person.

6.8 The Reporter is the official to whom all children thought to be in need of compulsory measures of care are referred, in the first instance, by doctors, health visitors, social workers, police officers, teachers or ordinary members of the public. Before making any decision in respect of a child, the Reporter is obliged to carry out such investigation as he may think necessary. He may refer a case to a Children's Hearing; he may take no further action; or he may decide that, although social intervention may be justified, such intervention need not necessarily be compulsorily imposed. In that event the Reporter may refer the child to the local authority with a view to their making arrangements for the advice, guidance and assistance of the child and his family on an informal basis.

6.9 The role of the Reporter is unique. Although employed by the local authority and accountable therefore to that authority for the satisfactory performance of his administrative duties, the reporter is completely autonomous in his decision-making functions with regard to children referred to him. Under statute, he alone has responsibility for determining whether to refer a child to a children's hearing or to choose another of the options open to him. In addition to this primary decision-making function the Reporter has a wide range of other duties including framing grounds for referral, arranging children's hearings and presenting cases before the sheriff on application or appeal. There are as yet no prescribed qualifications for Reporters and we understand that the introduction of the national training course, which was in prospect until recently, has yet again been deferred. Although many Reporters now in post have legal or social work qualifications a growing number of new entrants lack a relevant training on the scale proposed for the national training course and we strongly recommend that priority be given by both central and local government to establishing this course.

6.10 One of the most striking features of the hearing system is the way in which the needs of children are met by crossing professional boundaries. Reporters are in daily communication with many professional agencies in regard to children who have been referred to them as being in need of compulsory measures of care. The police, for example, may bring a child to the attention of a Reporter because of petty theft. On further investigation however, the Reporter may learn that, because of disruptive behaviour in school, the child has already been referred to a child psychiatrist or psychologist through the special education services. In such cases it is normal practice for the Reporter to seek reports from both of these agencies before coming to a decision as to whether the child might require compulsory measures of care.

6.11 Most Reporters have experienced a fall in the number of referrals from the police; in 1973 these accounted for over 80% of all referrals but fell to 59% of the total in 1981. On the other hand, referrals from social work departments, mainly involving children at risk of abuse or neglect in their own homes, more than trebled between 1973 and 1980. Given the general concern of all the agencies involved with such children, it seems likely that what has been recorded is not so much an increase in incidence as a better quality of surveillance on the part of the reporting authority. In most of these referrals, the issue is not a clear cut case of "non-accidental" injury but rather a manifestation of multifactorial neglect or of pervasive emotional deprivation. Many of the children concerned come from single parent families, where the adult is suffering from social isolation and loneliness as well as from emotional and economic stress. Alcohol-related problems, desertion and psychiatric illness frequently figure in the grounds of referral.

6.12 As the hearing system has developed, it has become possible to concentrate less on the presenting problem and to consider in more depth the individual needs of each child. The likelihood of an appropriate decision being taken on a child's future care or management depends on the extent to which there is a genuine dialogue between, on the one hand, the child and his parents, and, on the other, the professionals responsible for assessing his "treatment" needs. A children's hearing provides both the forum for such frank discussion, and the authoritative setting in which formal decisions can be taken. Conditions inserted into supervision requirements can be useful but must be feasible. For example, a condition that a child should undergo a period of psychiatric treatment would require the agreement of the psychiatrist concerned; similarly, a condition that a child should reside in a particular List D school would require the consent of the headmaster of that school.

6.13 The multidisciplinary approach to the plight of child victims of "non-accidental" injury, physical neglect or other abuse, was highlighted in the First Report of the Select Committee on Violence in the Family.[30] In most regions there are now liaison committees with a responsibility for considering matters of local policy on child abuse, and there are also multidisciplinary case conferences, whose purpose is to agree a suitable course of action in respect of any child who is at risk of ill-treatment or neglect in his own home and about whom there is shared concern.

6.14 Frequently a child referred to the authorised agencies may suffer from a mental disability. Such cases may be far from straightforward, especially where the child concerned is very young. As noted above, where a child is not capable of understanding the explanation of the grounds of referral to a children's hearing, the Reporter should be instructed to make application to the sheriff for a finding as to whether any of the grounds have been established in law.

6.15 In some cases a child's disability may have resulted from abuse or neglect on the part of his parents, one or both of whom may also suffer from mental disability. It is not uncommon for children's hearings to delay a decision about allowing a child to return to his parents' care, even under compulsory supervision, until there has been some investigation, psychiatric if necessary, into the mental state of the parent, or parents, concerned. This can be done however only with consent, since hearings have no power of compulsion over parents.

6.16 Under present legislation it is difficult for Reporters, in an application to the sheriff, to prove impairment of emotional health or development as an indication that the child may be suffering from a serious lack of parental care. Cases involving lack of parental care point to a need for supporting expert opinion to be led in evidence, as a means of interpreting for the court a series of facts, or a set of circumstances, which have been noted in professional workers' reports. Even then, sheriffs may not be persuaded that lack of care exists to the extent that serious impairment of mental health or development will occur at some future date. This is likely to be the case where there is contrary evidence which suggests that there has been adequate physical care of the child, and perhaps satisfactory educational attainment on his part. It is important therefore that such expert opinion, whether medical or social work, should include an authoritative interpretation of the facts of the case and a reasonably firm prediction about future risk factors. For a child who is not already under the formal supervision of the local authority, this evidence may be crucial to the provision of some form of legal protection since, if the case were proved, the sheriff would then remit it to a children's hearing for disposal.

6.17 Reporters are careful that information given to them about children is kept confidential within the system and there are statutory safeguards about the transmission of information contained in reports. Courts, too, are careful to protect, so far as is compatible with the interests of justice, the professional relationship between doctors and their patients.

6.18 Although the children's hearings system is at a relatively early stage of its development there is now a need for a wide-ranging and independent review of the system. This should take full account of recent research[31] and of the experience accumulated in operating children's hearings over the past decade. It should also be aimed at developing the system on sound welfare principles, rather than contracting it or attempting to make it revert to the more traditional form of juvenile justice.

7 Children away from home
I—Decisions and resources

7.1 We devote this chapter, and the subsequent four chapters, of our report to an examination of the different services which exist for children who do not live continuously with their own parents. There is substantial evidence that such children constitute a vulnerable group from the point of view of their mental health; and the type and quality of provision made for them will determine whether their prospects of healthy development are enhanced or put at greater risk. Indeed, an appropriate response by statutory and voluntary agencies at this stage may reduce the need for the provision of extensive social services at a later date. Although we are primarily concerned here with the nature of the alternative care provided for them, we are in no doubt as to the importance of the part played by the child and adolescent mental health service and by child guidance services, in regard to individual treatment and in relation to the provision of consultation and support to those concerned with alternative care.

7.2 While we have not given consideration to private boarding schools, those concerned with the running of these schools should be equally alert to the dangers of emotional deprivation and should be equally aware of the availability of services. We hope that the implications of our report will not escape the attention of head teachers and governing bodies of these schools.

7.3 Although neither this chapter nor the subsequent ones are primarily concerned with children away from home for the treatment of a physical condition, a high standard of child care is essential in all hospitals to which children are admitted, or which they attend as out-patients. Hospitals should have defined policies of child care, and the responsibility for their implementation should be clearly allocated. We draw attention yet again to the importance of open visiting by parents, and to the need for more facilities for parents to stay in hospitals to which younger children are admitted. We commend practices designed to reduce the level of all hospital admissions of children.

H.M.S.O. 3

7.4 We are concerned, when we speak of "children away from home", with a wide variety of situations, since separation between parents and children may be voluntary or involuntary, temporary, intermittent or long term. Accommodation provided not only by voluntary organisations, education authorities, and social work departments, but also by the National Health Service and the Prison Service is involved in housing children away from their parents. The precipitating reason for alternative care, away from the child's biological family, may be the child's disturbed or delinquent behaviour, or the inability of his family to provide continuing care for him. The objectives of alternative arrangements may be perceived differently by the child, his parents, those caring for him, the relevant professionals, and society in terms of punishment, deterrence, containment, assessment, treatment, education, training, specialist care or substitute parenting, A similar variation obtains in social attitudes towards the children concerned. Thus, whereas a child living in a children's home may be regarded as the victim of unfortunate circumstances, a pupil in a List G school as a recipient of the benefits of special education, and a young in-patient in a psychiatric unit as suffering from illness, a resident in a List D school will be perceived primarily in terms of his delinquency.

7.5 All moves into alternative care should constitute an improvement on the child's existing circumstances, and the care provided must be the best available for him. In any alternative provision, whether by the statutory authorities or by voluntary agencies, due regard must be given to each child's need for education, good physical and emotional care, and adequate control. Because of the many diverse routes by which children come into alternative care, and the different perceptions of the aims of such care, it is all the more necessary to take steps to ensure that each child receives the form of provision most suited to his needs. For example, those who make decisions in relation to children who have committed offences must strike a balance between the protection of society and the child's need; nevertheless, it is the child's eventual healthy development, and not necessarily the immediate reason for his referral, which must be the major factor in any decision as to where he is to live, either temporarily or permanently. The history of David illustrates the unhappy consequences for a child of disregarding this principle.

7.6 There are at present several different systems for allocating and maintaining specialised facilities through which alternative care is provided. Children with similar needs may thus be scattered across the range of available provision, while children with different needs who arrive by the same route (for example the children's hearings) at a particular type of provision may find themselves inappropriately placed together. In short, decisions about placement can be affected by extraneous circumstances which are quite unconnected with the child's needs.

7.7 Such extraneous circumstances can, in fact, determine the overall shape of residential provision; and, over the years, there has been a distribution of such provision which is now seen to be inappropriate in relation to present national and local needs. This is particularly true of the List D schools system (see paragraph 9.22). Another instance is the provision for mentally handicapped children, the number of children in hospitals for the mentally handicapped being chiefly a reflection of the inadequate level of provision made for them in the community. It is not enough that there should be a wide range of alternative care: facilities must be provided on the basis of a rational examination of the child's needs rather than on haphazard development by individual agencies.

7.8 There is, at present, no means available for estimating the numbers of children who move between health, education, social work and penal provision. Statistics of children living away from home are collected by a number of bodies and on different bases. The best estimate we could make of the total number away from home on any one day suggests that, in 1981 some 11,000 children or around 1% of the population under 18 in Scotland were in residential establishments run by social work departments or voluntary organisations, in foster homes or in care and placed with relatives, in List D schools, in residential special schools, in hospital wards, in adolescent units or in penal institutions. (Children living with adoptive parents have been excluded from the calculation.) These figures do not reveal how long the children concerned had been away from their parents on the date in question; they may represent continuous or intermittent periods from a few days to several years. The average length of stay, for instance, of children in a paediatric ward is a matter of days rather than weeks. Others may have experienced longer periods of intermittent or continuous alternative care, for example, about 10% of foster children spend more than five years with their foster parents. Particularly for young children, however, the significance of even short periods in public care cannot be discounted. It is essential, therefore, that reliable and comprehensive information is regularly available to indicate the extent to which children are placed away from home, both for long and short terms, and to show their movements between services of different types in different localities.

The decision to remove a child from home
7.9 We are agreed that, no matter which authority is involved:

(a) no child should be removed from his own home unless enquiries have clearly indicated that he cannot otherwise receive adequate assessment, care, treatment, education or control. The policy presupposes a range of services available and acceptable to the parents and the children including housing, income support, health, education, domiciliary provision, intermediate treatment and counselling. In this connection we welcome the introduction of schemes which provide care within the child's own home, or which may obviate the necessity for children to leave home; the Strathclyde pilot project, employing mobile care staff is one example; the provision of day schools for children with special needs, and of day facilities in assessment centres are others. It is totally unacceptable that children should be separated from either parent for no other reason than that the family is homeless;

(b) if, in an emergency, a child has to be removed from home immediately, whether or not on a Place of Safety Order, a full investigation should be undertaken without delay;

(c) no environment to which a child is moved, whether for a short, or a long, term should exist solely for containing or holding, no matter that such a function may sometimes be an inevitable component of the care provided in that particular setting;

(d) a full assessment of a child's physical, educational, emotional and social needs, and of the resources necessary and available to meet them, requires the skill of different disciplines. Such an assessment may be necessary when a child's move from home is under consideration, immediately after this has taken place, and at any subsequent time when a change of plan is envisaged.[32][33] It is important that there are adequate medical, educational, psychological and social work resources available and that the decision to assess a child should relate to the child's needs and not to the administrative category in which he has been placed;

(e) where it is intended that he should return to his family, the child and the family should be given practical help to enable them to preserve their links, and to help the family to make any changes in its circumstances which are thought to be in the child's interests;

(f) if it is unlikely that the child will return to his parents in the foreseeable future, this should be recognised quickly and realistic plans for his long term care made, and implemented, without delay;

(g) we stress again that every child should participate, within the limits set by his age and understanding, in discussions about plans for his future, as is required by the Children Act 1975, Section 79.

Assessment

7.10 Assessment may be carried out whilst the child remains at home, through his attendance at hospitals, clinics, day assessment facilities or intermediate treatment schemes, or alternatively on the basis of admission to an assessment centre or other residential establishment. Whether or not the child leaves home for this purpose, reports from the school and from social workers on interviews with his family are normally available.

7.11 As we have already indicated (para 7.9(a) above) a child should be admitted for assessment on a residential basis only if the enquiries necessary to a decision about his future cannot be adequately carried out while he remains in his current environment. We welcome the introduction of schemes for the development of assessment on a non residential basis. We believe that the child and adolescent centres referred to in Chapter 12 should promote the co-operation of professionals in inter-disciplinary assessment schemes and may provide a locus for day assessment facilities.

7.12 In some instances however it may be necessary for a child to be contained in a residential setting if he is to be assessed at all; in others the child and those who have been living with him may need a period of respite from each other during the assessment period; and for some children the facilities for continuous observation by skilled staff which some establishments offer may be a necessary part of the assessment process. These reasons for admission to an assessment centre appear to us valid. We are led to believe, however, that children are sometimes admitted to centres for punitive or deterrent reasons. This is not consistent with a regime which should be directed primarily to the understanding of children and of their circumstances. It has also been suggested that children are admitted for the greater convenience of the professionals involved in interveiws with the child. We do not regard this as a sufficient reason for removing a child from his home environment.

7.13 At present there are 14 residential assessment centres in Scotland. There is no standard definition of the functions of these centres and considerable variation in the way they carry out their work. As well as undertaking assessments in the main for children referred by Hearings, they may provide care for children on a short term or emergency basis, receive absconders from other establishments, accommodate children awaiting placement, and offer long term care. All the centres provide education on the premises and a few send some children to outside schools. Centres differ in their size and intake, in their resources, in the manner of their organistion and in their individual philosophies; the experience afforded to a child in one of these establishments is very much the product of these interrelated elements.

7.14 The number of children accommodated varies from one centre to another. Some restrict their intake to a particular age range and those admitting only older children may be dealing predominantly with young people who have committed offences. The ratio of residential social workers and teachers to children and the extent of their extraneous duties are also variable; in some centres many children receive only part-time education because of staff shortages. Centres differ also in their standards of furniture and equipment and in the amount of support provided by visiting consultants. In some centres, possibly as a consequence of their original function as remand homes, there still exist features characteristic of narrowly custodial regimes such as locked doors, exercise in an enclosed yard, institutional clothes, absence of possessions and regular searches of the person. Other establishments pursue a more child care orientated policy preferring to establish, by less formal regimes, closer relationships with the children.

7.15 We are concerned about the length of time some children are left in assessment centres. We understand that they often remain long after an assessment has been carried out because no vacancy can be found in the type of establishment or foster home which is considered to be most appropriate to their needs. This may be because the recommendations reached by the assessment meeting were unrealistic in terms of the currently available resources or it may be because of delay in making the arrangements. It has been put to us that availability of finance is in some areas an important factor in decisions about placements and also that problems arise because of the difficulty of obtaining vacancies in certain List D schools. Whatever the reason for the delay, the effect on a child of a prolonged period of uncertainty in a constantly changing group of children, and in what is essentially a temporary environment, cannot be other than disturbing.

7.16 We have noted that centres set up primarily for the assessment of children have come to serve many purposes, including the development of some programmes for long term care. There are obvious difficulties in providing regimes for short term assessment and for long term care within the same establishment but we are interested in the view that this can be successfully achieved if facilities for separate living are provided for the two groups and if the objectives for those retained for long term care are clearly defined and understood by all concerned. Because some anxiety has been expressed to us that a number of children are being accommodated on a long term basis in residential centres without any satisfactory arrangements for their education or rehabilitation we recommend that the use of long term units in assessment centres should be very carefully monitored.

7.17 The requirement in the Children Act 1975 that a local authority must take into account a child's wishes and feelings in decisions about his future underlines an important general principle. In the context of assessment it implies that the assessment team must consider carefully in every instance which person is to be responsible for helping the child to understand what is involved in assessment and to represent his point of view when decisions are made.

7.18 The teachers and residential social workers in assessment centres, because they are concerned with the changing population of children all at points of crisis in their lives, and because their professional observation of these children and their impact on them have important implications for the future, must be recognised as needing a high degree of skill and training.

7.19 Research is needed to evaluate, through the outcome of recommendations and the decisions to which these lead, the procedures adopted in assessment. (See chapter 14). It follows that, if the assessment processes currently in use in residential centres are found to be effective, they should be available for all children for whom important changes are envisaged and not confined, as now, largely to those who have come before a Children's Hearing.

8 Children away from Home
II—Fostering and Adoption

8.1 Fostering, unlike adoption, does not involve the permanent loss of the rights and duties of the biological parents, although once the Children Act 1975 is fully implemented, foster parents may more easily be granted legal custody. Foster care varies from the short-term placement of children whose mothers are in hospital, to long-term placement where children remain for many years in their foster homes and come to regard the foster families as their own. In addition to foster children who are in the care of voluntary organisations and those in the care of the local authority social work departments, others, who are privately fostered, are also subject to social work supervision. Among developments in fostering practice, which we welcome, are the fostering of mentally and physically handicapped children, either long-term or for regular holidays from hospital, the fostering of a child with the same family when the mother has to go into hospital repeatedly; the "alternative scheme" developed in Kent for adolescents who would otherwise be placed in residential establishments; and the "community parents" schemes in Strathclyde, Lothian and Grampian. We are particularly concerned that more schemes for offering training, and adequate remuneration, to foster parents should be developed.

8.2 As to private fostering, we have no means of knowing how far the unsatisfactory position described in "Trading in Children"[34] exists in Scotland today. This study showed that many privately fostered children, two-thirds of whom were under five, compared unfavourably, physically, emotionally and intellectually, with children living with their parents, or in local authority care. Although there is a statutory requirement to notify private fostering, there are well-recognised difficulties in ensuring compliance. More efforts should be made to collect up-to-date information about children in this group, whose mental health may be at risk. Those privately fostered children who are notified to local authorities should be properly supervised and protected. We recommend that Sections 95, 96 and 97 of the Children Act 1975, which relate to regulations for supervision by local authorities of private fostering, should be implemented without delay.

8.3 The traditional approach to home finding is to recruit potential foster parents, and then to attempt to match children to them. Recently, the press and sometimes television have been used to encourage potential parents to take an interest in particular children. Strathclyde's community parents project, the Barnardo's "adoption shop" at Colchester, the "new families" project in Glasgow and the London-based specialist adoption agency, Parents for Children, are examples of this approach. While the right placement is paramount, older children being fostered long-term should be placed so that the change in their environment is not too radical, and so that the placing agency's social worker can visit easily. There will always be some children, however, who cannot readily be placed locally, and for whom a suitable family could be found further afield. We commend, therefore, the arrangements which have been established to share these resources, notably the Scottish Resource Exchange, operating under the umbrella of the British Agency for Adoption and Fostering; and we hope that something will come of the proposal to establish an all-Scotland network.

8.4 An adoption order severs the legal relationship between the child and his biological parents and establishes a new legal relationship between him and his adoptive parents. At one time adoption was regarded primarily as a means of providing childless couples with healthy babies, but, in the past decade, experience in the United Kingdom and in America has shown that many older children and many handicapped children can be placed successfully. We recommend that the practice of providing long term home support for parents adopting difficult children should be considered in Scotland, initially as a pilot project. We recommend that those sections of the Children Act 1975, relating to the introduction of a statutory adoption service, should be implemented without delay.

8.5 Home finding, placement and continuing support in fostering and with adoptive parents require a high degree of social work skill. Whether or not the biological parents continue to be actively involved, the existence in a child's life of more than one set of parents can be stressful, both for the child and for the adults concerned. We welcome increasing specialisation, whether within area teams or in central units, in fostering and adoption, which we see as a means of improving the very variable quality and the lack of consistency of social work in this field. We believe, moreover, that all those engaged in this work, whether through voluntary or statutory agencies, should have ready access to expert support in social work departments, and that this support should be built up by planned experience and study, after qualification. Of course, it is not only social workers who are involved in placing children; others, such as members of those committees which consider applications and placements, may need help to acquire the understanding necessary to make the important decisions involved.

8.6 Successful home finding, fostering and adoption placement depend not only on the quality of staff but on the extent to which social work administrators and local authority members, recognising its importance, allocate staff time to this field. In the face of other urgent demands, such allocation may sometimes be difficult, but its long-term benefits must be stressed. At any stage of fostering or adoption, professional support must be readily available. Counselling may need to be supplemented by financial support, which can for instance assist in obtaining the services of a home help, especially in the initial stages of the fostering or adoption of handicapped children. Child and adolescent mental health services should make available support to foster parents, social workers and others who are concerned with fostering and adoption.[35]

8.7 On foster care, the "Guide to Fostering Practice"[36] identifies standards which, if they were generally adopted, would do much to promote the mental health of children in foster care.

9 Children away from Home
III—Varieties of Residential Provision:
Homes and Residential Schools

9.1 Residential accommodation is provided at present by local authority social work departments, education authorities and voluntary organisations. Such accommodation is variously designated and comprises children's homes, homes for mentally handicapped children, residential schools for children with physical, sensory and/or mental handicap and for maladjusted children, assessment or reception centres, List D schools and hostels. Childcare accommodation provided by voluntary organisations has to be registered with the local authority under the Section 62 of the Social Work (Scotland) Act 1963.

Staffing of Residential Accommodation

9.2 The staff of these homes, and other residential child care establishments, are part of the daily living experience of those for whom they care. Because of this intimate, sustained, contact they have a key role and can affect for good or ill the mental and physical wellbeing of the children and adolescents who live in homes, assessment centres, residential schools and hostels. Thanks to the increasing trend over the past twenty years, which has enabled children to remain where possible within their own families, those now admitted to any type of residential establishment are likely to present considerable problems. It follows that staff working in a residental setting require complex skills in providing care, assessment, control, treatment and social education for a group of children with special needs. Too often it is assumed that a warm heart and goodwill towards children are the only necessary qualifications for work of this kind. Although in recent years there have been some attempts to analyse the task of residential social workers in general[37, 38, 39, 40, 41, 42], there is still very little understanding of the task of the residential child care worker.

9.3 Both the form of training for residential child care workers, and the numbers of untrained staff now employed, give cause for serious concern. The Central Council for Education and Training in Social Work has decided that training for residential social work should be of the same length and standard as training for fieldwork, and should follow the same pattern. Special courses for residential workers are being replaced by combined courses for field and residential staff, leading to the award of the Certificate of Qualification in Social Work. Although we welcome this development, we are concerned that much of the work on many CQSW courses may continue to be focused on the area team, that insufficient opportunity may be available to students to acquire specialised knowledge about children, and that the skills of practice teaching in the residential setting may be underdeveloped. Moreover, the contribution of the new Certificate in Social Service, as a qualification for residential work with children, is still unclear. The existence of two different qualifications, both considered appropriate for work in a residential setting, implies a differentiation between social workers and other care staff in children's homes, which requires clarification. We welcome the enquiry in this area recently carried out by the Central Council for Education and Training in Social Work. We are in no doubt that the level of basic training for residential social work with children should be at least as high as for fieldwork; and, in the context of this report, we particularly wish to emphasise that any training for residential child care workers must include the development of knowledge and skills which will enable them to promote the mental health of the children in their care.

9.4 The latest statistics available from the Social Work Services Group[42] reveal that in homes for children and young people, the proportion of care staff with social work qualifications is very low.

9.5 It is not only in basic training that a considerable improvement is required. It is also necessary for those in management positions to have opportunities (such as barely exist in Scotland at present) for post-qualification study in child care.

9.6 The Williams' Report[43] showed that in 1967, in the average children's home, one third of the staff was replaced in a year. In that same survey it was noted that larger homes had to replace 40% of their resident staff and 75% of their non-resident staff each year. We understand that high rates of staff turnover continue to be a problem in children's homes.

9.7 The distress and disturbance caused to children by high staff turnover in children's homes cannot be over-emphasised; a child who is beginning to re-establish confidence in relationships with adults will find it difficult to bear the departure from the home of anyone with whom he as a close relationship. It is important to pay regard to this when temporary staff and students become involved with individual children. The recently improved salary structure for local authority residential staff, together with improved working conditions and the growing practice of living out may go some way towards remedying the problem of high staff turnover. Non-resident staff may be more stable in their jobs, and more involved with life in the community than staff who make their own home in a children's establishment. Nevertheless, it is important to recognise that these developments, and others already mentioned, contribute to the perception of children's homes as a preparation, rather than as a substitute for family life.

Children's homes

9.8 Children's homes are an important resource in Scotland. There is, however, a lack of clarity as to their function. This is often described solely in terms of the provision of physical care and "upbringing": and yet, at the same time, there has been, in recent years, much emphasis on the need of every child for a family of his own. The publication, in 1973, of "Children Who Wait"[44], drew attention to the plight of children remaining indefinitely in residential care, often for the greater part of their childhood. There are in Scotland many children who have already spent long periods in residential care and whose chance of successful family placement is consequently slight. It is important to recognise, therefore, that a residential establishment is likely to be the only home which these children will have while they are growing up. This means that, in addition to an environment which will prepare them for an independent life, they must also be provided with affection and stability.

9.9 Although many children still spend long periods in children's homes, the aim of rehabilitation with parents, or of placement with a family, carries the clear implication that the function of these establishments is not solely to provide a substitute home. A major element in their work is to prepare children, whose development and behaviour may have been adversely affected by past deprivation, for a return to some form of family life. Children's homes, therefore, in addition to effecting changes in children while resident, have a contribution to make during the transitionary periods following a child's admission to the home and leading up to his discharge. The residential social worker's part in helping children to come to terms with their continuing need for care, and with the possibility of moving to a permanent home apart from their parents, is a central one, which needs much greater recognition.

9.10 These functions of children's homes clearly indicate that they share major objectives with List D schools and residential schools for maladjusted children, since these establishments are likewise concerned with preparing children for family life or independent living in the community. It follows therefore that children's homes should be regarded as forming part of the range of specialist residential facilities required for children and young people.

9.11 Children's homes are too often regarded as self-sufficient units. If their central task is to prepare a group of children needing skilled help either for a return home or for family placement, they will need to work closely and continuously with field social workers and with psychologists, psychiatrists and educationalists. The staff in a residential establishment also need the support of an experienced residential social worker. Staffing ratios need urgent review, not only in children's homes and assessment centres, but also in residential schools, including List D schools. We recommend that the Secretary of State should institute such a review.

Residential educational provision

9.12 In addition to independent fee paying schools, there are residential schools for children with physical, sensory and/or mental handicap, and for maladjusted children. Residential provision is also made for those children who are considered to require placement in a List D school. We endorse the Warnock Report's recommendation that "where special school provision in the maintained sector is inadequate, as it is particularly for children with emotional or behavioural disorders and those with severe learning difficulties, it should be increased to the point of sufficiency". This report also pointed to the need for more flexibility in the use of residential accommodation, recommending that "a range of different types of boarding school should be available which would include not only residential special schools of the traditional type, but also schools which cater for children with varying needs for residential accommodation and education on or off the premises, including schools of the hostel type[20]. We agree with this approach.

9.13 At present the demand for some forms of residential educational provision exceeds the supply; this sometimes leads to children being placed in a school which simply happens to have a vacancy at the time, rather than in the most appropriate one. The residential schools in question are, moreover, unevenly distributed in Scotland, with the result that the children may be placed at a distance from their homes and their ordinary schools, with consequent difficulty in maintaining important links. All this leads us to the conclusion that, because of fragmented administration and funding, residential educational provision is not used to the best advantage.

9.14 The needs of most children are best met in two separate, but related, environments, namely the home and the school. For this reason we are agreed that children should be admitted to residential establishments with education on the premises only in the following circumstances:

a. where it is not possible to cater on a non-residential basis for highly specialist education requirements; or

b. where, because of a child's behavioural problems, or severe handicap, it is essential to provide integrated educational and care regimes, or

c. where his need for containment and control cannot be met when school and home are separate.

It follows that children should not be admitted to a residential school simply because they have to be removed from their own home. There is room, as we have already indicated, for the further development of children's homes and hostels to meet circumstances of this kind.

Current residential provision for physically handicapped and maladjusted children

9.15 The number of residential places required for physically handicapped children has, we are glad to see, decreased in the past decade, largely because more flexible provision has become available in day schools. In September 1982 there were 966 maladjusted pupils (all ages) in education authority and grant aided special schools. Of these, 379 were resident and 587 day pupils[45]. Maladjustment may also have been a factor in determining the need for residential provision in children suffering from other handicaps.

9.16 In a considerable number of cases, children considered to be maladjusted, and requiring education in schools for the maladjusted, are unable to live at home; and the need for residential places for such children remains consistently high. Pupils in this category vary from children whose educational or emotional difficulties have led to behavioural problems, to those whose gross deprivation has made it impossible for them to benefit from normal education and whose overall behaviour leads to difficulties for themselves and for others.

9.17 We have recommended that children with special educational needs should wherever possible attend specialist day schools, but this is not always feasible. Despite the small numbers involved, there are some disabilities where effective intervention demands a highly skilled service, with a high teacher pupil ratio and a complementary group of skilled residential child care staff. The needs of children in rural areas also require special consideration; and a small number of rare disabilities call for provision to be made on a regional or national basis.

9.18 It is wrong to place children whose difficulties stem from the nature of their social backgrounds in residential schools, which are often at a considerable distance from their own homes. Many children, who require the facilities of schools for the maladjusted but who cannot live at home, would be able to remain in their own locality if specialised hostels or children's homes were provided. Children who have benefited from a period of special schooling may continue to do well if they are returned to ordinary education; this is not feasible in every case, but such a course of action should be considered and adopted wherever possible.

9.19 All these residential schools should have a workable catchment area, so that families can be involved in children's care and rehabilitiation wherever this is possible. Where children are already in care, or where, even after intensive social work, there is no possibility of the family being able to provide the care and support necessary, it is essential to make consistent provision for holidays.

9.20 There is a shortage of places in day schools for children with difficulties. In some cases, pupils who could live in their own homes, or in children's homes, are admitted unnecessarily to residential schools. It adds to their problem for children already in group care, as in a children's home, to have to spend 40 weeks in the year in another group setting, even when they are able to return for holidays and weekends to their original base. It is seriously detrimental to the mental health of children in residential schools that they should have to spend their holidays and weekends in a series of different children's homes, or in assessment centres with their changing populations of residents.

List D schools

9.21 There are 21 schools currently grouped under the Scottish Education Department's List D, providing accommodation for 1,215 boys and girls. On 17 July 1983 there were 762 boys and 104 girls on the registers[46]. They vary in size, in the range of provision they offer and in the philosophy they adopt. The smallest school takes only 20 pupils, the largest 80; there is provision in three schools for secure accommodation; and one provides no education. They also differ from each other in the degree to which they emphasise the discipline and control elements in child care and development. The isolated geographical location of many of the schools, for which there were no doubt good historical reasons, now seems inappropriate and often makes contact with parents difficult. Where the schools are suitably placed in or near urban areas, useful experiments have been made, offering not only full-time residential care and day education, but also the options of education only, or residence only, while the child attends the local authority day school. We recommend that this flexible approach, which reflects the varying needs of individual children, should continue to be encouraged.

9.22 Children are admitted to List D schools in the following circumstances:

—on a residential supervision requirement made by a children's hearing (Section 44(1)b) Social Work (Scotland) Act 1968;

—under Section 206(2) or 413 of the Criminal Procedure (Scotland) Act 1975;

—on a voluntary basis under Section 15 and 16 of the Social Work (Scotland) Act 1968;

—on a voluntary basis through an education authority.

For children admitted through a children's hearing, the regional authorities pay a fee prescribed by the Secretary of State, based on 50% of the cost of keeping a child in a List D school. For children sent to such a school under the Criminal Procedure (Scotland) Act, the Scottish Education Department meets the final cost. When children are admitted on a voluntary basis, the regional authority, through the agency of the Director of Social Work or the Director of Education, as appropriate, pays a fee based on the full cost of accommodating children in a List D school. These anomalies in the payment of fees discourage some local authorities from placing children appropriately and according to their needs. No child should be denied appropriate residential care for purely financial reasons.

9.23 In most of the schools, children are now admitted under a form of "contract" between the social workers, parents, other interested agents and the child. This reflects the framework in which the children's hearing system works. "Contracts", which establish mutually acceptable agreements for admission are also used in some residential schools for the maladjusted. We recommend the continued development of admission procedures which are aimed at matching needs with the most appropriate available resources.

9.24 Although there has been no detailed research, as yet, on the characteristics of pupils admitted to List D schools as compared with those of children admitted to other residential establishments, the Working Party's report on "Educational Staffing Ratios in List D Schools"[47], concluded that there was no appreciable difference in the nature of the problems of the children admitted to either kind of establishment. We are of the view, therefore, that it is wholly appropriate to group List D schools with all other residential schools.

9.25 List D schools, like other establishments for troubled or troublesome children, provide a residential lifestyle in which processes of remediation and of readjustment can begin to take effect. The staff who live with these children need support; and the managers of List D schools need to maintain and develop their different ways of supporting staff.

9.26 Residential education should be developed as part of a coherent system through a joint local approach. List D schools have been a bone of contention for many years. They are centrally financed, but run, in the main, by voluntary organisations; they draw their intake from local authorities, but often from authorities other than those in whose areas they are located. While we appreciate the historical reasons for the present position, we believe that it is now essential to end the current isolation of the List D schools from the main stream of services for children and young people. We recommend that this should be achieved by their inclusion in a local pattern of residential services, with due allowance being made for cross-boundary flow between regions. Such a change might be difficult to effect, but it should not be impossible.

9.27 The necessary opening out of the List D "system" can be most effectively achieved by voluntary organisations and local authorities working in partnership to create regional plans for those now admitted to List D schools. We believe that such a joint approach would be more conducive to the further development of these schools than the system of central control has been, at least in the recent past. Not only would it help reduce the stigmatising and scapegoating effect of the schools' current isolation, it would also make it possible for the schools to retain their voluntary identity while, at the same time, forming an integral part of the local services for children and young people. The joint planning body to which we refer in Chapter 12 should review the place, in its range of services, of any List D school, or schools, in its area.

9.28 In recommending the development of this new framework for the care, education and control of difficult youngsters in residential care, we emphasise in addition to a continuing relationship between voluntary bodies and the Government, the need for an early shift towards greater co-operation with local authority social work and education departments; and the joint planning body, to which we have referred, should be prepared to co-opt members from the Board of Managers of a List D school, as and when necessary.

9.29 We also recommend that this joint planning body should consider the development of the psychological service for children, currently designated as the List D schools' psychological service, with a view to making this service more widely available. Many List D schools' psychologists already have important links with assessment centres and similar facilities.

Intermittent care

9.30 In paragraph 8.1 we mention the development of intermittent care within the same foster family for those children whose circumstances necessitate repeated periods away from home. Some children's homes and some List D schools have also successfully supported children through difficult periods by offering continued contact, and occasional direct care on a day, or temporary residential, basis. These are valuable initiatives which should be encouraged and, if possible, extended.

Neighbourhood short-term units

9.31 There may be a need in some areas for the provision of a small neighbourhood unit to provide counselling, day care and group activities for families at times of crisis, together with temporary accommodation for the children. Where parents and older children are in serious conflict, a short respite from the stress of living in close proximity with each other may avert the need for formal measures and perhaps for prolonged separation. We see these neighbourhood units as family first-aid posts, available on demand, but referring, as appropriate, for long-term intervention, and enforcing time-limits in relation to their residential provision.

9.32 We recommend that, at the earliest opportunity, a small number of such short-term neighbourhood units should be set up on an experimental basis, the value of their contribution to be carefully monitored.

10 Children away from Home
IV—Severely Disturbed Adolescents

10.1 Voluntary organisations, social work departments, the NHS and the education authorities provide a wide range of services for disturbed adolescents. Most of these young people are helped through brief intervention. Some need more than this, and a number are admitted to residential establishments. Of this number, the majority adapt without difficulty to the regimes maintained in these establishments, but some, of whom Danny (see the Prologue) is an example, become a source of concern because of (a) the problems of managing them, (b) their impact on staff and on other residents, and (c) their need for specialised help if their future is not to be bleak. Opinions vary widely, both about the severity and the extent of the problems presented by severely disturbed adolescents, and about the kind of provision which should be made for them. In our view, this troubled, and often troublesome, minority have rarely had a fair chance and, since their early experiences have been almost invariably appalling, we are particularly concerned that they should be given a better opportunity in adolescence. This is why we consider them separately at this point in our report.

10.2 In the last 10 years, 13 patients aged 16 or under have been admitted to the State Hospital at Carstairs. Of these, 9 came through the courts and 4 from other hospitals. More research is needed into the characteristics of those who need an intensive care unit. The following factors are relevant and merit further study:

—actual, or potential, excessive violence;
—creating fear of violence among staff caring for them;
—self injury;
—uncontrollability;
—unpredicatability;
—repeated absconding.

Although we have referred to violence, and the fear of violence, society is still ambivalent about the management of these young people, and remains undecided about the best combination of control and care.[48, 49] It is important to bear in mind that the precise characteristics of severely disturbed youngsters are difficult to define. They are not distinguished by the type of offence which they commit, by the amount of actual violence to which they resort, or by their background. They appear to be more readily defineable, first, in terms of the emotional reactions which they create in the staff of the various institutions, and, secondly, in terms of the extent to which such staff fail to achieve control over them. In short, violence is often the outcome of relations between staff and children, and its presence may tell us as much about the institutions in which it occurs as about the young person concerned. Moreover the actual incidence of violence is low; and it is significant that a comparatively small number of institutions in England and Wales make use of the Youth Treatment Centres which have been set up south of the border.

10.3 Special provision for the kind of children under discussion has been made in at least one List D school, namely, Kenmure St Mary's. These arrangements have worked successfully and should be further evaluated.

10.4 We are satisfied that there is a pressing need for a unit providing intensive support for severely disturbed young people, who are a danger to themselves or to others, and serving the whole country. We are aware that such a unit may be set up in a number of different ways, but in view of the need for early action, we recommend that the intensive support unit, which we have in mind, should be set up by the NHS near an existing adolescent unit in Glasgow or Edinburgh.

10.5 In this unit, the peer group experience could be used creatively to allow difficult youngsters to live together more successfully and to acquire a greater understanding of the needs of other people. At the same time, the staffing structure and social environment of the unit would require to be such that control was maintained, with ultimate authority residing in the staff.

10.6 Experience at Youth Treatment Centres indicates that children of both sexes can be accommodated together in such units very successfully. Given the need for close relationships with staff and the problems of dealing with large groups, the number of highly disturbed children who can be satisfactorily cared for in one unit must be limited. A unit size of between ten and twenty places is probably ideal. The age range of the children in the unit should not be too wide.

10.7 To allow for progression during the child's period of residence, the unit would need a flexible range of treatment programmes. Programmes of behaviour modification, and of training in social skills, are relatively new innovations, both of which have something to offer. The integration of different types of treatment programmes so that they can work harmoniously however requires a high degree of expertise. Many of the young people in a unit for those whose behaviour is severely disturbed will require long periods of care and treatment; and some of them might eventually need to be transferred to a mental hospital. At the same time, there are others who may benefit in a matter of months. When a further lengthy period in the unit is likely to produce only minor benefit, then clearly transfer to another placement would need to be considered.

10.8 The broad range of educational and therapeutic experiences which we envisage for young people admitted to the unit would call for a wide range of staff, including psychiatrists, nurses, residential and field social workers, teachers and psychologists. These staff would be employed by, or seconded to, the NHS. The unit would also require an administrator with specialised skills and appropriate training. A high staff/child ratio would be important, not only because of the valuable contribution which it would make to security, but also because it would make it easier for the children to form attachments which could be developed and built upon.

10.9 The unit would also need access to other resources, for example, education, recreation and employment, both for children able to go out from the unit and for those confined within it. It would also need to develop links with a wide range of other services, in institutions and in the community, so that suitable placements could be found for children ready for discharge. Amongst those admitted to such a unit, there might be children with brain damage and epilepsy whose disturbed behaviour was largely the result of their physical condition; from time to time these children would need specialised medical treatment.

10.10 It would be necessary for the families of such children to establish new relationships with them so that while the children will acquire relative autonomy, their family links, potentially the best support system of all, would be maintained and strengthened rather than weakened. In general, parents should be regarded as having a positive part to play in relation to their children's needs in the unit. At the same time, we recognise that some parents might be so inadequate or incompetent as to require support and encouragement, while a small minority might turn out to be so harmful that they should not continue to be involved.

10.11 It is particularly important that the unit should be so placed as to make it possible for children to relate to a community, particularly in respect of their education, employment and possible future long-term placement or residence.

10.12 We have given careful thought to physical security, since this is essential in the case of some disturbed youngsters, not only to protect the outside community but also to meet the needs of the children themselves. Security however must be a servant, not a master; and given that other controls may often be more effective, its use by staff should be flexible. We appreciate, of course, that in order adequately to provide for the needs of severely disturbed children, staff must have confidence in their ability to cope with them. The mere fact that they are working under conditions of physical security can sometimes remove anxieties and contribute to their sense of confidence.

10.13 It is likely that the staff of such an intensive support unit would be called upon to provide a consultative service to other institutions experiencing difficulties in managing individual children. An important function of the unit should be the provision of a setting for joint training of all the professions involved with young people whose behaviour is severely disturbed. We have no doubt that two-way arrangements of this kind would help to reduce the need for such young people to be admitted to the intensive unit.

10.14 Closed units may have negative aspects and the work of the intensive support unit which we envisage should be monitored and, if necessary, legislation should be devised to protect the rights of the young people referred to it.

Penal provision

10.15 We believe that a considerable number of older teenagers, sentenced in the courts to periods of imprisonment in young offenders' institutions, or to borstal or detention centre training, have previously received some form of alternative care, with or without special education. The incidence of psychiatric disturbance in younger childhood has long been known to bear some relationship to deviance and delinquency in the late teens and in early adult life.[50] Accurate information about the numbers of teenagers in young offenders institutions, borstals and detention centres who have had periods of alternative care is impossible to obtain. We recommend that a study of the previous experience of public care among young people in this category should be undertaken, with a view to identifying any changes in services which might reduce the need for penal provision in the older teenage group.

10.16 From time to time some children under 16 convicted of an offence and committed for residential training by a court are sent to penal establishments. These places are made available, usually on an interim basis, by the Secretary of State where social work departments have made a strong case. The determining circumstances are mainly the lack, at the time, of other appropriate residential provision. After assessment, nearly all of these youngsters are transferred to List D schools or other establishments. Only a very small number remain in penal establishments for the period of their training, and generally these are aged 16 or over. Normally every effort is made to find a placement which meets the needs of those children for whom the Secretary of State is responsible, and the overriding aim is that, as far as is reasonably possible, such children should be kept out of penal establishments. We strongly support this approach; and recommend continued effort to provide additional alternatives to penal provision, so that, in time, its use for children will become unnecessary.

11 Children away from Home
V—Keeping Track and After-Care

Keeping track of children in long-term care

11.1 In examining existing provision for children away from home we have become aware that the needs of an individual can become lost in a maze of organisational complexity. As we have already indicated, it is often the particular label first attached to a child—disturbed, delinquent, maladjusted, in need of care—which determines the agency which provides for him, the nature of the assessment processes through which he passes, and the environment to which he is moved—all this although the administrative label may not be an accurate indicator of need. In any case, the regimes of certain assessment centres, child psychiatric units, List D schools, residential schools and children's homes have more in common with each other than they have with some other establishments in the same official category. We are concerned, too, that a child in "alternative" care may well pass several times to different placements under the same agency, from one type of organisation to another, or between two similar agencies in different parts of the country. Beset by a multitude of demands to be met from limited resources, authorities often have great difficulty in pursuing continuously the interests of any particular child. Again, because of high workloads and low staffing levels, an excessively long time may be taken to reach a decision about a child, whose important developmental needs remain unmet. These problems can all be compounded by the frequency with which some families move.

11.2 It is also a matter for concern that some children may still remain in residential establishments for a long and indefinite period. Although the cases of those who have appeared before a children's hearing and are subject to a requirement of supervision are reconsidered at least annually, the children themselves being involved in this review, and although the Education Act requires children with special educational needs to be reviewed, no similar statutory requirement applies to other children. We recommend that Section 80 of the Children Act 1975, by which all children in the care of local social work authorities will be subject to a six-monthly review, should be implemented without delay. It must be said, however, that, although useful, such reviews do not, in themselves, necessarily lead to action. For this reason, we have examined other possibilities.

11.3 We first considered the case for a national reviewing body, transcending all existing agency boundaries, which would maintain a national register of all children away from home for more than six months or who have had three or more periods in public care. A duty would be imposed on all authorities running residential establishments or responsible for other alternative care arrangements to give the body information about children within these categories in their care, and to report any change in a child's location or in the agency responsible for him. Such a review body would be responsible for monitoring the welfare and progress of children on the register, and have power to investigate and act if necessary. We then went on to consider a proposal for the creation of a multidisciplinary regional review committee, with similar powers and duties. Although there was some support for both of these proposals, we do not think that either would be feasible, or, indeed, desirable, at the present time. Our concern about the dangers to children of being lost in, or between systems operated by large corporate bodies nevertheless remains; and we feel that a greater awareness of children's needs on the part of all professionals involved, as well as the maintenance of high standards of work by the managers of every agency responsible for children, would go a long way towards providing a remedy.

11.4 The question then arises as to how this greater awareness might be fostered. After considering the problem in some depth, we recommend that every child away from home for more than six months, or on three or more occasions, should be the assigned responsibility of a designated professional within the agency currently responsible. (For children in residential special education, this responsibility already rests with the principal educational psychologist.) The individual so designated should be at a level carrying authority over the major resources for children within the organisation, and he or she should be of sufficient status to negotiate appropriately with other authorities whose services may be necessary to the child. Each designated professional would be accountable for monitoring the welfare of the children so assigned, would have a duty to pay proper regard to their physical, social, emotional and educational development, and would be responsible for ensuring that the child was transferred to a similar agent if, on discharge, another public body took responsibility for him. Since the person designated to carry out those responsibilities may well occupy, within the agency, a position which excludes regular, direct work with children, we also recommend that, in these circumstances, each child should have, in addition, a named professional key worker to carry out direct work with him (including the ascertainment and consideration of his wishes and feelings at all times) and to ensure the implementation of any agreed plans. This key worker should known by, and be acceptable to, the child and should retain contact with him for as long a period as possible.

After-care

11.5 We are concerned that many children and young people leave long-term care to live in unsatisfactory home situations, and are deprived at the same time of any kind of continuing support. For young people, the continuing high level of unemployment exacerbates the resultant problems of loneliness, alienation and a sense of worthlessness. It is totally unacceptable that the most careful assessment and treatment of a child while he is in care is frequently thwarted, afterwards, by the lack of any continuing professional concern.

11.6 If there is not a suitable home in the community available to him, no young person should be obliged to leave long-term residential care merely because he has reached a certain age; and greater attention should be paid, while children are still in residential establishments, to preparing them for life outside after their discharge. We recommend that, at the crucial point of discharge from care, a named social worker (residential or field) should be given the responsibility of being available to the young person for at least two years, or more, depending on his or her maturity. The use, explored by some authorities, of volunteers in relation to children leaving long-term residential care may be particularly helpful, but it still requires careful evaluation. In Chapter 4 we referred to the need for accommodation, in some instances with additional support, for young single people. Those passing out of the long term care of local authorities are in particular need of facilities of this kind and we believe that social work departments should recognise their responsibility to ensure that appropriate provision is made for them.

11.7 We were pleased to learn of a number of informal "contact points" where young people leaving care can continue to meet, and where there are social workers available. Such meeting places provide opportunities for practical and emotional support, thereby giving young people a sense of belonging and of being needed; they can also be of use in facilitating the detection of early warning signs in the case of children who need further help. We recommend the further development, where the need exists, of such informal meeting places.

12 Organising for the Future

12.1 The skills which are required to cope with the complex problems arising in mental health work with children are spread throughout a number of different disciplines and a number of different agencies. Although it is not, in itself, a sufficient, it is nevertheless a necessary, condition of further progress in this field, that these skills should now be promoted within a different framework. We are convinced that a more interdependent system of working must be developed, through which the different agencies and professions involved may reach agreement on objectives and co-ordinate contributions towards their achievement. This will not only give valuable support, and a fresh stimulus, to professionals, voluntary workers and administrators, but will also help to eliminate or reduce gaps and overlaps in provision and thus enable the best use to be made of scarce resources. We have noted that some joint working does take place at present, but where this happens it is often at a purely personal level. Conflicting approaches compounded by organisational fragmentation, (in particular separate budgets, different administrative hierarchies, procedures and priorities, and the employment of the various categories of professional staff by different authorities and agencies) can defeat the best intentions of those involved in providing mental health services to children and young people.

12.2 Inevitably, under the influence of historical factors and specific local needs, different ways of working together, both at the inter-professional and at the inter-organisational level, will develop in different situations. However, there are certain broad criteria, relating to different, inter-locking, organisational levels, which, in our view, cannot be ignored:

—The child and his family must be included in inter-professional decisions about his future;

—First line collaboration, between doctors, teachers, health visitors, social workers and others in the promotion of prevention and the provision of help, should have an emphasis on co-ordination of effort rather than mere co-operation.[28][51] This will depend on the development of a supportive organisational structure, which enables the different professionals involved to commit themselves to inter-professional work;

—This supportive structure should begin at the level where resources are being committed to the implementation of policies. There should be established by health, education and social work agencies, in partnership with any voluntary body concerned, arrangements which will facilitate the agreement of detailed objectives by these agencies, and the collaboration required for their achievement;

—Matching of stategies at area/regional level can be effective only if liaison committees between health boards and local authorities are under-pinned by joint planning arrangements of the kind referred to in the Warnock Report,[20] with voluntary agencies involved where appropriate;

—The need for improved co-ordination between Ministers and between the central departments concerned with services impinging on the personal development and mental health of children and young people cannot be over-emphasised. A number of Departments in the Scottish Office and elsewhere for example, the Department of Health and Social Security, are involved in activities which are directly or indirectly relevant to the needs of children, since wider social policies in housing, planning, income maintenance and employment may have an impact on the way families are able to function. Insofar as the mental health of children and young people is concerned, it is important that these Departments should be working within policy frameworks which are, as far as possible, compatible with each other. We hope that, as well as keeping in close touch with his Ministerial colleagues, the Scottish Minister with the primary interest in this particular client group will be able to designate a lead Division in the Scottish Office with authority and responsibility for maintaining and developing liaison, and joint working, within and between Departments. Only when services are planned, managed and delivered on an integrated basis, and only when there is national leadership to that end, can the best use be made of limited resources. We welcome recent initiatives between Departments, in areas relevant to our concern, as important first steps towards the more positive arrangements for collaboration within the Scottish Office, which we consider to be essential;

—Provision must be made for evaluation in the light of agreed priorities. In addition to being regularly monitored by the professionals and agencies involved in their delivery services relevant to the mental health of children and young people should be kept under periodic review by a suitably representative body set up for this purpose.

12.3 We are aware that the arrangements for co-ordination of the kind which we propose may raise considerable problems, in regard both to administrative and financial procedures, and to the provision of an appropriate information base for inter-dependent services. Since our proposals do not encroach upon professional independence, or upon the separate identities of the different agencies involved, we hope that, given the political will to improve services for children and adolescents, these problems will not prove insuperable.

Child and Adolescent Centres

12.4 A major element in the proposed inter-professional and inter-agency collaboration, would be the setting up of multidisciplinary child and adolescent centres, which would function as the main foci of the child and adolescent mental health services.

12.5 Child and adolescent centres should be associated with particular localities, should serve identified communities varying in size but preferably not exceeding a population of 200,000 and should be so located that access to them is not a problem and that they, in turn, are well-placed to play a full part in early detection, follow-up and evaluation.

12.6 The functions of these centres would be as follows:

—to provide a comprehensive range of assessment, treatment and support, both by using their own services and by facilitating links with others known to them locally. These services would be provided to children and adolescents in the environment in which they normally live. Referrals would be taken from general practitioners, schools, staff in social work departments, voluntary organisations, children's hearings and other sources in the centres' localities.

—to act as a major resource for professional and administrative training and to make available advice and support to individuals and bodies concerned with children in the community;

—to collect and analyse data relating to problems arising in the areas served by the centres, and to provide a specifically child and adolescent mental health orientated perspective for the benefit of policy-makers.

12.7 At the inception of a centre, its professionals should, as a matter of priority, negotiate with staff in child guidance and child psychiatric services the extent to which these services should be provided within the centre. There would be no question of dismantling the existing forms of provisions. Rather we would see the child and adolescent centre as a focal point for the different services currently involved, and as a way of increasing their effectiveness. We envisage that over time there would be some rationalisation of the pattern of referrals to these services, and that this would simplify their individual tasks, although some re-allocation of resources might be necessary between agencies.

12.8 We do not envisage a residential, or in-patient facility at the centres; those needing residential treatment would be referred to hospital departments, or places sought in residential schools, assessment centres, children's homes or foster homes.

Staffing of Child and Adolescent Centres

12.9 Child and adolescent centres would require to be staffed by a multi-disciplinary group. These professionals should have a major commitment to the centre, working there for a substantial part of their time. They should, however, continue in employment with their parent agencies, retaining full professional and organisational links with their colleagues there.

12.10 The professional group should comprise a child and adolescent psychiatrist, a clinical psychologist, an educational psychologist, an appropriately qualified social worker and a nurse with experience in this field.

12.11 Other professionals having working links with the centre would include general practitioners, paediatricians, general psychiatrists, clinical medical officers, health visitors, reporters to children's panels, residential and field social workers, and guidance and other specialist teachers. Voluntary workers would also be appropriately involved; and each centre would need an administrator, and secretarial and reception staff.

Administrative Arrangements for Child and Adolescent Centres

12.12 We wish to emphasise the need for flexibility in the setting up of child and adolescent centres in different parts of the country. Such centres would not necessarily need purpose-built accommodation, but could be set up in whatever accommodation, and under whatever administrative arrangements, were locally considered most appropriate. They could possibly, for example, be associated, when local circumstances permitted, with the handicap centres proposed in "Towards Better Health Care for Children at School".[17] We recommend that, in the first instance, two or three pilot projects should be initiated in different parts of the country (if necessary with the help of support financing) and thereafter carefully evaluated.

13   Staffing and Training Requirements

13.1 Child and adolescent mental health, including as it does aspects of health, social work and education, is a rapidly developing field. We feel that ways should be found, during the 80s, of improving the relevant services, and the staffing implications of our report, and the training needs of staff, must be a paramount consideration for health boards and local authorities.

Staffing—Doctors

13.2 We have made reference in Chapter 5 to the broad scope and growing importance of the work of child psychiatrists, and we have referred throughout the report to different areas in which child and adolescent psychiatrists will be required to develop services, along with colleagues from other professions. We consider that present staffing levels in child and adolescent psychiatry are inadequate to cope with these pressures. On 30 September 1981, there were in post 29 consultants (28.1 full-time equivalents) and 16 senior registrars (13.6 full-time equivalents). The DHSS target for child and adolescent psychiatrists' staffing in England and Wales is one consultant per 200,000 population. Although that overall ratio has been achieved for Scotland, it does not apply evenly across all areas. Moreover, the Royal College of Psychiatrists recommends that 1½ consultants, together with junior staff, represents a realistic minimum for a population of 200,000.[52] To achieve this level of staffing, a 25% expansion of the consultant establishment is required. While the senior registrar establishment appears at first sight to be adequate, we recommend that it should be kept under close review, bearing in mind the established senior registrar training programmes in several parts of the country. In order to take into account the needs of part-time medical trainees, who, we envisage, may be increasingly attracted to child and adolescent psychiatry, we recommend that senior registrar training be made readily available on a part-time basis.

13.3 Some post-graduate training in child and adolescent psychiatry is also required by general practitioners, hospital and community paediatricians, and doctors who are to be involved in the care of children with mental handicap. Such post-graduate training needs, referred to in the Warnock and Court Reports, lead us to recommend a small increase in registrar staffing in child and adolescent psychiatry.

Nurses

13.4 We have already referred to the need for major improvements in the field of child and adolescent psychiatric nursing. The Report, "Towards an Integrated Child Health Service" pointed to the need for "positive therapeutic nursing care" of the mentally ill, or mentally handicapped, child.[53] We refer below to the training needs of nurses in the child and adolescent mental health services. Of equal importance is the need to clarify the nurse staffing requirements of these services. There is no nationally agreed method for estimating these. We consider that the overall nurse/patient ratio in psychiatric units for children and adolescents should be of the order 1.5:1.0, which provides for a working ratio of approximately 1:3 by day and 1:6 by night. We recommend that the staffing situation in such units should be examined as a matter of urgency, with the aim of remedying deficiencies as soon as possible. Child and adolescent psychiatric nursing should, however, be extended from in-patient units to out-patient and community services. Although the most urgent need is for the development of training programmes, we recommend that, as these are developed, and as qualified nursing staff become available, a number of pilot projects should be set up to establish the most effective use of child and adolescent psychiatric nurses outside residential units. Such pilot projects might be set up in association with the child and adolescent centres which we have recommended. We recommend, too, that in order to raise significantly the quality of care and training, nursing officers should be enabled to continue in the child and adolescent mental health field.[54] The future level of health visitor staffing should take into account the developing roles of health visitors in the field of child and adolescent mental health. We recommend that health visitor staffing should be of the order of 1:3,000 population.

Clinical Psychologists

13.5 In 1980 there were 28 clinical psychologists specialising in work with children and young people in Scotland. We agree with the recommendation of the Clinical Psychology Sub-Committee of the National Consultative Committee of Scientists in Professions Allied to Medicine, based on experience in health boards which supply a service in this field, that this establishment should be increased to 60.

Educational psychologists

13.6 In 1974 the Scottish Education Department stated that a ratio of one educational psychologist to 3,000 of the school population would enable child guidance services to function effectively.[55] The Warnock Report recommended a ratio of 1:5,000 of the total child population from birth to 19 years in England and Wales—a trebling of their staffing level to a position rather more favourable than the Scottish ratio of 1:3,000 of the school population. The Peters' Report[16] recommended a ratio for Scotland of 1:2,500 of the school population by 1985.

13.7 In an analysis of the situation, psychologists have noted that since many of these estimates were made, the range and quantity of work undertaken by the child guidance services in Scotland has expanded greatly. They have suggested that, for services which are becoming increasingly community orientated, a ratio to the whole population might be considered as more appropriate than one related only to part of it. A recent estimate made by them of the optimum needs of a particular child guidance service resulted in a proposed ratio of one psychologist to 10,000 of total population.

Social workers

13.8 We recommended in para 5.23 that each child and adolescent mental health service must maintain an appropriate involvement of social workers. We recommend further that where more than one social worker is involved, one of them should be of senior social worker grade: where only one is participating, he or she should have several years' experience. There should, additionally, be a minimum establishment of one social worker to each consultant psychiatrist appointment. We also recommend that the Secretary of State should set in progress a review of staffing ratios in residential establishments for children.

Secretarial staff

13.9 Full-time secretarial staff are key figures in departments of child and adolescent psychiatry and, as they undertake a wide range of administrative and organisational functions, we recommend that the senior member of each department's secretarial staff should be appointed at Higher Clerical Officer grade.

Training

13.10 The major problem which has been brought to our attention relates to the unsatisfactory and isolated arrangements, in the child and adolescent mental health services, for training different groups of professional staff. (A significant exception is the Joint Curriculum and Training Group set up recently by CCETSW and the three nursing Councils following a request from the Government to consider the training of staff caring for mentally handicapped people in residential accommodation.) It is clearly beyond our present remit to give detailed guidance on the technicalities of such a complex field. We recommend, therefore, that a working party should be set up as soon as possible, representative of the professions and training institutes concerned, to undertake a review of existing training arrangements, both as to content and organisation, in order to effect the improvements in these arrangements which we consider to be necessary.

13.11 Without wishing to pre-judge the way in which such a working party might set about its task, we hope that it would take particular account of the following considerations:

a. **Focus of training**

Training should be based, as far as possible, on the needs of children and young people rather than on the aspirations and interests of the professions involved. The priorities should be:

    i. the promotion among professionals of a common understanding of the development of children and adolescents in the context of their families and of the wider social environment, with special attention being given to prevention and early detection, and to the needs of children and young people in institutional settings;

    ii. the provision of opportunities for professionals to learn about each other's roles and values and about the conditions which make for successful inter-professional co-operation;

    iii. the simultaneous deepening and sharpening, through contact with other professionals, of the individual's appreciation of his own professional skills, and of his ability to apply these skills.

b. **Interprofessional training**

Some rationalisation of existing training arrangements is essential. If the present lack of co-ordination is to be overcome, there must be a substantial element of inter-professional training in all academic and in-service courses. Courses organised on an inter-professional basis, or having an inter-professional element, provide an invaluable opportunity for members of the different professional groups to get to know each other and to learn about each other's work. Moreover, even short courses of one to three weeks' full-time study, or their part-time equivalent, can be an extremely effective way of helping professionals:

—to focus on broad, overall issues[51]
—to build up a common language for dealing with these issues
—to develop mutual understanding and inter-professional confidence and trust
—to develop their own particular professional skills through a dynamic process of role-blurring and role-clarification
—to agree on common objectives and to evolve inter-related responses to complex problems
to make the best use of scarce resources.

Medical students

13.12 The field of child, adolescent and family psychiatry is a developing speciality in which medical undergraduates need a thorough grounding. In the absence of academic departments of child and adolescent mental health in three of the four Scottish Medical Schools—we have recommended that steps should be taken to rectify this situation as soon as circumstances permit—a considerable burden of medical undergraduate teaching falls on NHS staff. Other University departments, including general practice, social medicine and social work, may also have a part to play; and this should be borne in mind when planning medical undergraduate teaching in child and adolescent mental health.

General practitioners

13.13 There is a special need to offer general practitioners on vocational training courses posts in child and adolescent psychiatry (ideally family psychiatry), as an alternative to the adult psychiatric experience now included in the general practitioner training programme. This training would certainly be as relevant to general practice as that which is given in adult psychiatry.

Nurses

13.14 It is essential that nurses in the child health services should be able to recognise emotional abnormality and they must therefore be given adequate preparation through appropriate training. Even if this was given due attention in general, paediatric, mental and mental deficiency nurse training this would not adequately prepare the nurse for giving specialist care to disturbed children or adolescents. We recommend therefore that the development of the child and adolescent psychiatric nursing service should be vigorously promoted by the provision of suitable post-registration courses. At least one such course should be set up immediately; the course successfully conducted at Newcastle provides a model[56].

Occupational therapists

13.15 Occupational therapy students are rarely given experience in child psychiatry. Such a specialised area warrants post-qualification training.

Social workers

13.16 Whatever the setting within which they work, social workers should receive appropriate training for working with children and those who care for them. We are aware that opportunities for specialisation are now developing in the basic qualifying courses, but many of those undertaking important work with children and their families have not specialised in this way. In any case, we are doubtful as to the extent to which existing opportunities for specialisation offer adequate preparation for all social work with children. We are glad to learn that CCETSW has been considering issues of specialisation in courses for the CQSW.

13.17 We have already drawn attention to the particular training needs of residential social workers, and we support the policy of CCETSW in promoting training for residential social work within CQSW courses. An analysis of the complex skills involved in residential work with children, and the ways in which they may best be developed, is beyond the scope of this report, but further enquiry in this area is urgently necessary. The question of differentiation between the work appropriately undertaken by CQSW and CSS holders in this context should be further pursued by CCETSW, employing authorities and the professional associations.

13.18 Post-qualification courses in social work with children, adolescents and their families should always be available, particularly for all those occupying, or about to occupy, specialist posts. The present pattern of basic training for social work makes the provision of such courses doubly necessary.

Educational psychologists

13.19 A wide variety of practical skills is now demanded of educational psychologists. In order better to equip them to adapt to changing tasks in child guidance, there is a need to reform existing training. An improved programme of training is required such as that set out in a recent report by the psychologists' associations[57]. This takes account of the need for the psychologists to develop skills with children individually and in groups and with the adults involved with them, including not only parents but other professionals, whether these professionals are part of the child guidance service of members of other agencies. We were glad to learn that new proposals are under discussion between the psychologists' associations and the employing authorities.

Short-term intensive training courses

13.20 The inadequate training of staff caring for children in residential settings calls for an immediate response which should not prejudice the introduction of long-term courses. The most feasible and effective means of compensating for past neglect, and of developing interprofessional training in the immediate future, is likely to be through short courses, whether full-time or part-time. Accordingly we recommend that short inter-disciplinary, in-service training courses should be set up in response to local needs, as soon as is reasonably practicable. Such courses could be organised through the collaborative arrangements which we have recommended in Chapter 12.

Training and research functions of the child and adolescent mental health service

13.21 Two important elements of the work of the child and adolescent mental health service are teaching and research. The teaching commitment, although steadily growing, is often informal (eg in-service courses for field and residential social workers, foster parents, children's panel members and others) and only one medical school in Scotland, the Glasgow Medical School, has a Department of Child and Adolescent Psychiatry, although this is a speciality which is distinct both from general psychiatry and from child health: for, although child and adolescent psychiatrists, rightly or wrongly, receive much of their professional training in general psychiatry, in practice they work more closely with the rest of the child health service.

14 Research

14.1 There is a great need to promote research into disturbances of mental health in children and adolescents, and their families, and to identify research areas which should be accorded a high priority in the future.

Areas in which research is needed

14.2 Our deliberations have led us to conclude that the following areas should receive priority when consideration is being given to the development of research programmes.

(i) A detailed study is required to ascertain how methods of ameliorating disturbances of mental health of children and adolescents can be made simpler and more effective, and how they can be more widely delivered. We consider that a study should be made of methods used in primary schools (including involvement of voluntary workers) to promote socialisation and reduce behaviour disturbance in children starting school; and that there should be much more evaluation of techniques of intervention and treatment as used by specialised services on the one hand, and by primary health and social care workers on the other. Since methods of service delivery in Scotland at present differ considerably from one area to another, there is scope for comparative studies. The different ways of managing disturbed children and adolescents in the absence of in-patient facilities, and the differential use made of in-patient units for pre-adolescent children throughout Scotland, are also matters which would repay investigation.

(ii) We consider that work is also required to clarify the effect on the mental health of children and teenagers of marital breakdown, and to examine more closely the circumstances which help to protect children from impairment of mental health as a consequence of such breakdown. In this context, an examination of the factors in Scottish schools which influence learning and behavioural difficulties should be extended to the examination of the ways in which schools can support children who are in difficulties at home.

(iii) The optimum level of specialised alternative care, residential and non-residential, for troubled and troublesome children and teenagers in a given area is far from clear. A systematic examination of this matter, perhaps in two areas of Scotland, one urban and the other rural, should provide useful information for planners in regard to capital and revenue expenditure on alternative care for such children, and it should also help to identify gaps or overlaps in present provision.

14.3 An academic department of child and adolescent psychiatry is established in the University of Glasgow. The establishment of such departments in the other three Scottish medical schools would provide further opportunities for research in child and adolescent mental health. In the meantime, however, research in this field is initiated and supported financially by a wide range of agencies; and the responsibility for determining priorities in research is not located in any one body. In "Two Reports on Research into Services for Children and Adolescents"[58] the Joint Sub-Group on Behavioural and Emotional Disturbance in Children and Adolescents recommended that DHSS should consider the creation of a new multidisciplinary research unit "to undertake many of the important epidemiological and, hence, long-term projects required in order to provide a basis of knowledge for more applied research in service evaluation". We commend this approach for the United Kingdom; but we also consider that there is a need in Scotland for the identification of programmes and projects which could usefully be developed, and for the dissemination of research results, if necessary through officially sponsored research seminars. We hope that SHHD and SED will be able, first, to agree priorities for research in this field, secondly, to identify programmes and projects to be initiated and supported, and, thirdly, to keep future developments under regular review.

15 Summary of Principal Conclusions and Recommendations

Major recommendations are printed in italics.
Major recommendations with substantial resource implications
are underlined.

Chapter 1: Introduction

1. No previous attempt has been made by an official agency in the UK to produce a report encompassing the wide variety of services involved in the mental health of children and adolescents, with particular emphasis on the relationship between these services (para 1.1).

2. It is anomalous that the mental health of children and young people has not attracted the same degree of concern as has their physical health (para 1.2).

3. Because of our concern for the promotion of mental health, and of normal development, in children and adolescents, our focus has been on mental health rather than on mental illness (para 1.4).

4. We consider that the maintenance of close relationships between the different workers, both professional and voluntary, in this field, and between the different agencies involved, is crucial to the successful functioning of mental health services for children and young people (para 1.5).

5. We have not been wholly constrained by current stringencies and have interpreted our task as being that of providing a coherent strategy for the next ten years (para 1.6).

Chapter 2: Psychosocial Disturbance in Childhood and Adolescence

6. Disturbances of childhood and adolescence, unlike most psychiatric disorders in adults, are more specifically linked to development and must be seen, therefore, in the context of the normal development of mental health in this age group (para 2.4).

7. The majority of emotionally disturbed children can be treated by professionals other than psychiatrists (para 2.4).

8. The effective management of disturbances in children, and especially in adolescents, requires an understanding of the underlying factors behind expressed symptoms (para 2.5).

9. A single type of "symptom" can carry different significance at different ages and in different situations (para 2.5).

10. In the child and adolescent mental health services we are concerned with almost one third of the population of Scotland (para 2.7).

11. It has been estimated that approximately one child in ten aged 11 in Scotland is likely to be disadvantaged, as against one in 16 for Great Britain as a whole. On a low estimate, 6.8% of children aged 9-11 suffer from psychiatric disorders of sufficient severity to handicap them considerably (para 2.9).

Chapter 3:   Family, Neighbourhood and Community

12. The family (however formed) is still the key setting for normal emotional, cognitive and psychosocial development and the child's developmental needs are, to a considerable extent, provided from within the family (paras 3.2 and 3.3).

13 Stresses which occur in the life of all families are accentuated by disadvantage (para 3.7).

14. There are a number of protective factors, such as good schooling, improved family circumstances, etc, and the inherent resources of the family are of basic importance. The aim of services should be to reinforce the family capacity to fulfil its essential functions, with the minimum of outside help (paras 3.8 and 3.9).

15. It is also important, particularly in areas of multiple disadvantage, that the resources of the local community, and its capacity for self-help, should be mobilised to the fullest possible extent (para 3.10).

16. Voluntary help could usefully be extended in relation to the behaviour and socialisation of children starting school (para 3.15).

17. Every effort should be made to involve non-statutory agencies, and the community itself, in the planning, management and delivery of services (para 3.16).

18. *Effective prevention often depends on changes in the broader cultural environment and in appropriate legislative support. Educational policies should be directed towards public awareness of the real needs of children and young people; and much greater regard should be paid to the effect on child and adolescent mental health of planning and housing, as well as fiscal and economic policies (para 3.17 and 3.18).*

Chapter 4: The Mental Health Needs of Each Age Range

19. Ways must be found whereby the various services in this field can both increase their particular skills and, at the same time, develop their capacity to work together (para 4.1).

20. The already substantial contribution to prevention made by the primary health care team and other first-line agencies must be increased (para 4.3).

21. Effective parenting is crucial to the mental health of children and adolescents: increased health education in schools in planning for parenthood is necessary (paras 4.4 and 4.5).

22. Readily available and easily accessible family planning services continue to be essential and links between these services and the child and adolescent mental health services should be fostered. In appropriate cases, the importance of offering referral to a genetic counselling service should be kept in mind (para 4.6).

23. We welcome the attention now being paid by the obstetric and midwifery professions to the significance of the process of attachment between parents and child, starting with the first post-natal contacts. The mental health aspects of this process may all too easily be overlooked, and maternity services should be made aware of the contribution which can be made by consultation with the child and adolescent psychiatric services (paras 4.7, 4.8 and 4.11).

24. In the pre-school years, the mainstays of health care, in addition to the parents themselves, are the primary care team and the local child health clinics and community paediatric services, the health visitor being a key figure. Her importance in relation to child and adolescent mental health is not yet sufficiently recognised (para 4.12).

25. Infant mental health is a little-explored field. The child may often be a barometer of the family's health and this deficiency should be remedied (para 4.13).

26. All pre-school provision should be readily available, as accessible and attractive as possible and there should be a wider awareness of the fact that all services for pre-school children have a mental health component (para 4.14).

27. The value, in this field, of "developmental screening", and of "at risk" registers, has still to be established by further research (para 4.15).

28. *There is a growing conviction that the participation of parents and of the community, in pre-school provision is of fundamental importance (para 4.16).*

29. *It should be a duty of education authorities to make provision for children in their areas below the age of five who are found on assessment to have special educational needs (para 4.17).*

30. We recommend the further development of the pre-school programmes run by the child guidance services (para 4.18).

31. Services provided by registered child-minders are a potentially valuable addition to the range of resources available for family support. These services should not be limited to the under-fives (paras 4.19 and 4.21).

32. Parents should be involved in all pre-school day care establishments, and the question of mandatory pre-school provision should be re-examined (para 4.22).

33. Increasing attention must be paid to methods of improving the co-ordination of services for the under-fives and of ensuring their responsiveness to the needs of the community (para 4.23).

34. *Each pre-school child needing specialised services should have a specific, named person who would advise the family and help them in dealing with the different procedures and agencies (para 4.25).*

35. Training courses should be so designed as to enable teachers to make the fullest possible contribution to the mental health of children. Teachers should be closely involved in decisions about children with problems which are affecting their mental health or social and educational development (para 4.26).

36. Much joint effort is necessary to ensure that facilities and services are matched to the needs of children and young people (para 4.27).

37. Primary teachers, in particular, should regard it as legitimate to focus their own assessment skills on individual children, extending the circle of consultation as necessary (para 4.28).

38. Families coping with a mentally handicapped, or a "gifted", child need special support (para 4.29).

39. *We welcome the Warnock Committee's suggestion, now incorporated in the Education (Scotland) Act 1981 of a named person to provide a point of contact for the parents of every child who has been discovered to have a disability, or who is showing signs of special needs or problems (para 4.30).*

40. Mental health services for children and adolescents should when appropriate be provided through schools (para 4.31).

41. An evaluation should be carried out into the work of the type of units recommended in The Pack Report (para 4.33).

42. *Although special units may be necessary in some situations for children who can no longer be contained within the mainstream of the school, the "assessment panel" approach, based on the promotion of flexibility in time-tables, commends itself to us, but needs to be evaluated (paras 4.34 and 4.35).*

43. Education authorities should provide day schools for maladjusted pupils of primary and secondary school age (para 4.36).

44. The adverse effects of stress on teachers need to be further examined and there is a strong case for the development of an occupational health service for teaching staff as a partial solution to this problem (para 4.37).

45. The issue of control within schools requires to be considered in terms of the wider issues concerning control and responsibility in families, and in the wider community (para 4.38).

46. *The educational system needs to be adapted to achieve a better balance for all pupils of academic, vocational, practical and social subjects to prepare them for a full life in an increasingly complex society (paras 4.39 and 4.40).*

47. "Age breaks" in schooling can pose problems if there is insufficient preparation for change (para 4.42).

48. *It is important to link schools with parents and with the community. Experiments to this end in community schools, and in community education*

centres within existing schools, should be encouraged (paras 4.43, 4.44 and 4.47).

49. In areas of deprivation, links between the teacher and the social worker are particularly valuable (para 4.47).

50. *The basic concern must be with a wide concept of education which would have the aim of helping children to grow up into adults who can respond maturely and flexibly to a complex environment (para 4.49).*

51. It is essential to develop further statutory and voluntary schemes to help meet the needs of school leavers, and further research should be carried out on the impact of unemployment on the mental health of young persons in their late teens (para 4.51).

52. High priority should be given to the housing needs of homeless young people (paras 4.52-4.54).

53. Counselling services, in addition to the ordinary health education programmes, should be available to adolescents (para 4.55).

Chapter 5:   Services for Children and Young People

54. *There must be a new emphasis (which will have training and educational implications) on prevention in the primary care team and a recognition, at the same time, of the need to involve psychiatrists, psychologists, psychiatric nurses, social workers and others in first-line care (paras 5.2-5.5).*

55. The role of educational psychologists has expanded and their aim now is to facilitate the optimum development—intellectual, emotional and social —of children and young people from 0-19 years. Additional commitments are substantially changing the role of educational psychologists both within the educational system and in the wider field of child care provision. These developments are to be welcomed (paras 5.6-5.8).

56. The work of area social work teams has obvious implications for the mental health of children and young people. There is a need, therefore, for the further development of relevant post-qualification and in-service training (para 5.12).

57. The growth of intermediate treatment has been slow and piecemeal. Potentially it is a valuable addition to the range of services, but intermediate

treatment programmes must be carefully planned in consultation with other agencies, and they must be evaluated (paras 5.16 and 5.17).

58. The contribution of the voluntary sector is extremely valuable; a continuing partnership between statutory and voluntary services is needed (para 5.18).

59. Child and adolescent psychiatric services in Scotland are unevenly distributed (para 5.20).

60. A local child and adolescent psychiatric service should have attached to it a full-time senior grade clinical psychologist, one of whose functions should be to establish effective communications with the local authority's educational psychologist (para 5.24).

61. Child psychology should be a specialty within generic clinical psychology (para 5.24).

62. The nurse's part in therapy in child and adolescent psychiatry is not always fully recognised. Suitable post-registration courses should be provided and a sufficient number of specialist career grade posts should be created to ensure the development of greater nursing expertise in this area (para 5.25).

63. Occupational therapists, speech therapists, physiotherapists and dieticians have a particular contribution to make to the work of child and adolescent psychiatric teams (para 5.26).

64. Teamwork should be based on mutual respect, a sharing of skill and knowledge, and appropriate leadership. All the professional and voluntary workers in the child and adolescent mental health service should have a significant element of their training specifically concerned with work in multidisciplinary groups (paras 5.27-5.29).

65. In-patient provision for psychiatrically disturbed adolescents should be provided, integrated into a comprehensive child and adolescent psychiatric service (para 5.30).

66. When the condition of a mentally handicapped child is predominantly a behaviour disorder, or other psychiatric state, clinical responsibility should lie with the child and adolescent psychiatrist, who should also provide a consultative service to the paediatric service and to other agencies concerned with mentally handicapped children (para 5.31).

67. *The traditional medical base of the child and adolescent psychiatric service must be broadened. In particular, the psychiatric, psychological and social work components of the service should be united in a single area-based child, adolescent and family development service (para 5.32).*

68. The provision by child and adolescent psychiatrists of consultative services to other professionals and to the different agencies concerned with children and young people has staffing implications and there is an urgent need for a joint review by health boards and local authorities of the staffing needs of the child and adolescent mental health services (para 5.33).

69. *Out-patient services for children and adolescents with psychiatric disorder should be developed on the basis of an integrated, interdisciplinary team providing a co-ordinated service from common premises (para 5.34).*

70. In-patient treatment for pre-adolescent children should be provided in the ratio of 20 beds per 250,000 child population with this target being adjusted as appropriate to take account of local conditions (para 5.35).

71. In-patient provision for psychiatrically disturbed adolescents should be made, in the ratio of 18 beds to 250,000 child population, again with adjustment as appropriate to meet local needs.

72. Teaching and research in child and adolescent psychiatry are both seriously inadequate. As soon as resources permit, Departments of Child and Adolescent Mental Health, closely associated with existing Departments of Child Health, should be established in the three Scottish Medical Schools which are at present without such departments (para 5.37).

Chapter 6. Children's Hearings

73. The positive approach embodied in the concept of children's hearings is potentially more sensitive to the child's individual needs than traditional procedures (para 6.2).

74. As a further safeguard against any necessary erosion of a child's personal liberties on the grounds of welfare considerations, it is recommended that Section 66 of the Children Act 1975 be implemented at an early date (para 6.7).

75. It is strongly recommended that priority be given to setting up at an early date the national training course for Reporters, already agreed in principle by all the interested parties (para 6.9).

76. It is sometimes difficult, however, to persuade the courts that, where physical care is satisfactory, the mental health of a child may still be at risk. It is important that such expert opinion, whether medical or social work, should include an authoritative interpretation of the facts of the case and a reasonably firm prediction about future risk factors (para 6.16).

77. *There is now a need for a wide-ranging and independent review of the children's hearings system, which would take full account of recent research and of the experience accumulated over the past decade (para 6.18).*

Chapter 7. Children Away From Home
I—Decisions and Resources

78. Children who do not live continuously with their own parents constitute a vulnerable group from the point of view of their mental health; and the type and quality of provision made for them will determine whether their prospects of healthy development are enhanced or put at greater risk (para 7.1).

79. Hospitals should have defined policies of child care, and the responsibility for their implementation should be clearly allocated (para 7.3).

80. The importance of open visiting by parents is stressed: there is a need for more facilities to be provided for parents to stay in hospitals to which younger children are admitted (para 7.3).

81. Practices designed to reduce the level of all hospital admissions of children are to be encouraged (para 7.3).

82. *All moves into "alternative care" should constitute an improvement in the child's existing circumstances, and the care provided for him must be the best available. It is the child's eventual healthy development, not the immediate reasons for his referral, which must be the major factor in any decision as to where he is to live (para 7.5).*

83. Decisions about placement can be affected by extraneous circumstances which are quite unconnected with the child's needs. Facilities must be provided on the basis of a rational examination of the child's needs (paras 7.6 and 7.7).

84. *It is essential that reliable and comprehensive information is regularly available to indicate the extent to which children are placed away from home, and to show their movements between different services (para 7.8).*

85. No child should be removed from his own home unless he cannot otherwise receive adequate provision; and no environment to which he is moved should exist solely for containing, or holding (para 7.9).

86. If, in an emergency, a child has to be removed from home immediately whether or not on a Place of Safety Order, a full investigation should be undertaken without delay (para 7.9).

87. In order to arrive at a full appreciation of a child's needs, adequate medical, educational, psychological and social work resources must be made available at the assessment stage (para 7.9).

88. *Every child should participate, as far as possible, in discussions about plans for his future (para 7.9).*

89. *A child should be admitted for residential assessment to one of the 16 existing (and very differently constituted) centres in Scotland, only if the enquiries necessary to a decision about his future cannot otherwise be adequately pursued (para 7.10).*

90. Children should not be left in centres long after assessment has been carried out (para 7.15).

91. *The use of long-term units in assessment centres must be carefully monitored (para 7.16).*

92. The assessment team must consider carefully in every case which of its members is to be responsible for helping the child to understand what is involved in assessment and to represent his point of view when decisions are made (para 7.17).

93. Assessment should not be confined to those who have come before a Children's Hearing (para 7.19).

Chapter 8. Children Away From Home
II—Fostering and Adoption

94. More schemes should be devised for offering training, and adequate remuneration, to foster parents (para 8.1).

95. Although there is a statutory requirement to notify private fostering, there are difficulties in ensuring compliance. Information about privately

fostered children requires to be collected; and sections 95, 96 and 97 of the Children Act 1975 should be implemented without delay (para 8.2).

96. Recent attempts to match foster parents to children (instead of vice versa) are welcome. The arrangements established through the British Agency for Adoption and Fostering, and the proposal to set up an all-Scotland network, are to be commended (para 8.3).

97. There should be a pilot experiment in providing long-term home support for parents adopting difficult children (para 8.4).

98. *The sections of the Children Act 1975 relating to the introduction of a statutory adoption service should be implemented without delay (para 8.4).*

99. Increasing specialisation in fostering and adoption is an important means of providing expert support and improving social work practice and local authority decision-making in this field (para 8.5).

100. Child and adolescent mental health services should provide support to foster parents and to all those who are concerned with fostering and adoption (para 8.6).

101. The "Guide to Fostering Practice" identifies standards which should be generally adopted (para 8.7).

Chapter 9. Children Away From Home
III—Varieties of Residential Provision:
Homes and Residential Schools

102. All staff working in residential settings require complex skills; a warm heart and goodwill towards children are not enough (para 9.2).

103. *The level of basic training for residential social work with children should be at least as high as for fieldwork; and any such training must help residential social workers to develop skills which will enable them to promote the mental health of the children in their care (para 9.3).*

104. *Staff in management positions should have opportunities for post-qualification study (para 9.5).*

105. The distress and disturbance caused to children by high staff turnover in children's homes cannot be over-emphasised (para 9.7).

106. There is a lack of clarity as to the functions of children's homes, which are an important resource in Scotland. As well as being actively prepared for the time when they will live independently, children resident in these homes must be enabled to live as normal a life as possible (para 9.8).

107. The residential social worker in a children's home has a central role which needs much greater recognition (para 9.9).

108. Far from being self-sufficient units, children's homes must work closely with field social workers, psychologists, psychiatrists and educationists (para 9.11).

109. *We recommend that the Secretary of State should set in progress a review of staffing ratios in residential establishments for children (paras 9.11 and 13.8).*

110. There must be an adequate range of residential educational provision for children with emotional or behavioural disorders, and for those with severe learning difficulties. This is not the position at present; and, because of fragmented administration and funding, the existing stock of residential educational provision is not used to the best advantage (paras 9.12 and 9.13).

111. Children should not be admitted to a residential school simply because they have to be removed from their own home (para 9.14).

112. Children with special educational needs should whenever possible attend specialist day schools, but this is not always possible. Particular consideration should be given to the organisation of provision for them in rural areas, and a small number of rare disabilities call for regional, or national, provision (para 9.17).

113. Children whose difficulties stem from the nature of their social backgrounds should not be placed in residential schools; and, wherever possible, children who have benefited from a period of special schooling should be returned to ordinary education (para 9.18).

114. All residential schools should have a workable catchment area (para 9.19).

115. The shortage of places in day schools for children with difficulties should be remedied (para 9.20).

116. For children in residential schools, where holidays and weekends cannot be spent at home, there must be proper provision for holidays which does not involve the use of an ever-changing series of children's homes, or assessment centres (para 9.19 and 9.20).

117. Where List D schools are in or near urban areas, they have shown themselves capable of great flexibility; and this should be encouraged (para 9.21).

118. Existing anomalies in the payment of fees to List D schools should be resolved. No child should be denied appropriate residential care for purely financial reasons (para 9.22).

119. Admission procedures to List D schools which aim, through the use of "contracts", at matching needs with the most appropriate available resources, should be encouraged (para 9.23).

120. Managers of List D schools must maintain and develop their staff support systems (para 9.25).

121. Residential education should be developed as part of a coherent system through a joint local approach. The current isolation of List D schools should be ended and, under the joint planning arrangements to which we refer in Chapter 12, there should be a review of the place, in the local range of services, of any List D school in the area covered by these arrangements (paras 9.26 and 9.27).

122. *Members of the Board of Managers of a List D school should be involved in the joint planning arrangements referred to in Chapter 12; and while there may be a continuing relationship between voluntary bodies and the Government, there is a need for an early shift towards greater co-operation with local authority social work and education departments (para 9.28).*

123. The List D schools' psychological service should be made more widely available (para 9.29).

124. Some children's homes and some List D schools have successfully supported children through difficult periods by offering continued contact, and occasional direct care on a day, or temporary residential, basis. There are valuable initiatives which should be encouraged and, if possible, extended (para 9.30).

125. A small number of short-term neighbourhood units should be set up on an experimental basis (paras 9.31 and 9.32).

Chapter 10.   Children Away From Home
IV—Severely Disturbed Adolescents

126. Opinions vary widely about the problems presented by severely disturbed adolescents and about the kind of provision which should be made for them. Because of their usually appalling early experiences this troubled, and often troublesome minority, should be given a better opportunity in adolescence (para 10.1).

127. The actual incidence of violence is low and its presence may tell us as much about the institution in which it occurs as about the young person concerned (para 10.2).

128. There is a pressing need for a unit in Scotland providing intensive support for severely disturbed young people. A unit in which ten to twenty difficult young people could learn to live together and, at the same time, acquire a greater understanding of the needs of other people should be set up, near an existing adolescent unit in Edinburgh or Glasgow (paras 10.4-10.6).

129. *In the interests of security, and to help the children form attachments, a high staff/child ratio in the unit would be essential and it would need a broad range of staff, together with access to external resources (para 10.8).*

130. Although there will be exceptions, parents should be seen to have a positive part to play in relation to their children's needs in the unit (para 10.10).

131. The children in the unit should be able to relate to the local community in respect of education, employment, etc (para 10.11).

132. Security must be a servant, not a master; and its use by staff should be flexible (para 10.12).

133. The work of the unit, which would include the provision of a consultative service to other institutions, should be monitored and, if necessary, legislation should be devised to protect the rights of the young people referred to it (paras 10.13 and 10.14).

134. A study of the previous experience of public care among young people in penal institutions should be undertaken with a view to identifying any changes in services which might reduce the need for such provision among older teenagers (para 10.15).

135. Additional alternatives to penal provision should be provided so that, in time, it need no longer be used for children (para 10.16).

Chapter 11.   Children Away From Home
          V—Keeping Track and After-Care

136. *The needs of the individual child away from home can become lost in a maze of organisational complexity (para 11.1).*

137. We recommend that section 80 of the Children Act 1975 should be implemented without delay (para 11.2).

138. *Every child away from home for more than six months, or on three or more occasions, should be the assigned responsibility of a designated professional within the agency currently responsible. Such a child should also have a named professional key worker to carry out direct work with him (para 11.4).*

139. It is totally unacceptable that the most careful assessment and treatment of a child while he is in care is frequently thwarted, afterwards, by the lack of any continuing professional concern (para 11.5).

140. If there is no suitable home for him in the community, no young person should be obliged to leave long-term residential care merely because he has reached a certain age (para 11.6).

141. Greater attention should be paid, while children are in residential establishments, to preparing them for life outside after their discharge (para 11.6).

142. *A named social worker should be given the responsibility of being available to a young person being discharged from care for at least two years, or more, depending on the child's maturity (para 11.6).*

143. Informal "contact points", which provide opportunity for support and act as an early warning system in the case of children who need further help, should be encouraged (para 11.7).

Chapter 12.   Organising for the Future

144.   *The skills which are required to cope with the complex problems arising in mental health work with children are spread throughout a number of different disciplines and a number of different agencies. A more inter-dependent system of working is required, for the promotion of these skills, the identification of objectives and the co-ordination of contributions towards their achievements. It would also help to eliminate or reduce gaps and over-laps in provision and thus enable the best use to be made of scarce resources (para 12.1).*

145.   While different ways of working together may develop, we believe the following criteria must be met:

a.   The child and his family must be included in interprofessional decisions about his future.

b.   First line collaboration, between doctors, teachers, health visitors, social workers and others should have an emphasis on co-ordination of effort rather than more co-operation.

c.   This supportive structure should begin at the level where resources are being committed to the implementation of policies.

d.   Matching of strategies at area/regional level can be effective only if liaison committees between health boards and local authorities are under-pinned by joint planning arrangements of the kind referred to in the Warnock Report.

e.   The need for improved co-ordination between Ministers and between the central departments concerned with services impinging on the personal development and mental health of children and young people cannot be over-emphasised.

146.   *In addition to being regularly monitored by the professionals and agencies involved in their delivery, services relevant to the mental health of children and young people should be kept under periodic review by a suitably representative advisory body set up for this purpose (para 12.2).*

147.   The main focus of child and adolescent mental health services should be multidisciplinary child and adolescent centres located in the community (paras 12.4 and 12.5).

148.   The functions of child and adolescent centres would be:

a. To provide a comprehensive range of assessment, treatment and support to children and adolescents in the environment in which they normally live.

b. To act as a major resource centre for professional and administrative training and to make available advice and support to individuals and bodies concerned with children in the community.

c. To collect and analyse data relating to problems arising in the areas served by the centres, and to provide a specifically child and adolescent mental health perspective for the benefit of policy makers (para 12.6).

149. The core staff of a child and adolescent centre (ie the staff with a major commitment to the centre, working there for a substantial part of their time) should be a child and adolescent psychiatrist, a clinical psychologist, an educational psychologist, an appropriately qualified social worker and a nurse with experience in this field (para 12.10).

150. In the first instance, two or three pilot centres should be set up and carefully evaluated in different parts of the country (if necessary with the help of support financing) (para 12.12).

Chapter 13.   Staffing and Training Requirements

151. The staffing implications of the report, and the training needs of staff must be a paramount consideration for health boards and local authorities (para 13.1).

152. A 25% expansion of the establishment of consultant child and adolescent psychiatrists is required. The senior registrar establishment must be kept under close review, with senior registrar training being readily available on a part-time basis (para 13.2).

153. There should be a small increase in registrar staffing in child and adolescent psychiatry (para 13.3).

154. In in-patient psychiatric units for children and adolescents the nurse/patient ratio should be of the order of 1.5:1.0 (para 13.4).

155. Child and adolescent psychiatric nursing should be extended to out-patient and community services (para 13.4).

156. Nursing officers should be enabled to continue in the child and adolescent mental health field (para 13.4).

122

157. The future level of health visitor staffing should take into account the developing roles of health visitors in the field of child and adolescent mental health. We recommend that health visitor staffing should be of the order of 1:3,000 population (para 13.4).

158. The establishment of clinical psychologists specialising in work with children and young people should be increased to 60 (para 13.5).

159. The expansion in range and quantity of work undertaken by the child guidance services has staffing implications. For increasingly community-orientated services a ratio related to the whole population would be more appropriate than an establishment linked only to the school population. This would require a substantial increase in the number of educational psychologists (paras 13.6 and 13.7).

160. Each child and adolescent mental health service must maintain an appropriate involvement of social workers. We recommend that where more than one social worker is involved, one of them should be of senior social worker grade: where only one is participating he or she should have several years' experience. There should additionally be a minimum establishment of one social worker to each consultant psychiatrist appointment (para 13.8).

161. *Full-time secretarial staff are key figures in departments of child and adolescent psychiatry. We recommend that the senior member of each department's secretarial staff should be appointed at Higher Clerical Officer grade (para 13.9).*

162. *The unsatisfactory and isolated arrangements for training different groups of staff are a matter of concern and a working party should be set up as soon as possible to undertake a review of existing training arrangements with a view to improving them (para 13.10).*

163. Training should be based, as far as possible, on the needs of children and young people rather than on the aspirations and interests of the professionals involved (para 13.11).

164. *If the present lack of co-ordination is to be overcome, a substantial element of inter-professional training in all academic and in-service courses will be necessary (para 13.11).*

165. *Child, adolescent and family psychiatry is a developing specialty in which medical undergraduates need a thorough grounding (para 13.12).*

166. *There is a special need to offer general practitioners on vocational training courses posts in child and adolescent psychiatry (para 13.13).*

167. *Suitable post-registration courses should be provided for nurses (para 13.14).*

168. *Post-qualification training in the field of child and adolescent mental health should be available to occupational therapists (para 13.15).*

169. *Social workers should receive specialised training for working with children and it is imperative that post-qualification courses in social work with children, adolescents and their families should be available (para 13.16-13.18).*

170. The question of differentiation between the work undertaken by CQSW and CSS holders needs to be further pursued by CCETSW (para 13.17).

171. *The existing training of educational psychologists needs to be reformed to equip them for their changing task in child guidance (para 13.19).*

172. Without prejudice to the introduction of basic long-term change in training, short interdisciplinary in-service training courses should be set up in response to local needs through the collaborative arrangements recommended above (para 13.20).

Chapter 14. Research

173. There is a great need to promote research into disturbances of mental health in children and young people and to identify research areas which should be accorded priority (para 14.1).

174. Three areas for research we have identified are:

a. A study to determine how methods of helping disturbed children and adolescents can be made simpler and more effective, and how they can be more widely delivered.

b. A study to clarify the effect of mental breakdown on the mental health of children and teenagers, and to examine the circumstances which help to protect children from impairment of mental health as a consequence of such breakdown.

124

c.   An examination of specialised alternative care, residential and non-residential, for troubled and troublesome children and teenagers, with a view to establishing the optimum level of such care, and to identifying gaps in present provision (para 14.2).

175. The proposal that a multi-disciplinary unit be set up, to carry out research in the field of child and adolescent mental health in the UK is commended (para 14.3).

176. *There is a need for the identification of programmes and projects which could usefully be developed in Scotland. SHHD and SED should agree priorities, identify programmes and projects and keep future developments under regular review (para 14.3).*

BIBLIOGRAPHY

1. World Health Organisation (1977). Child Mental Health and Psychosocial Development. (Technical report series 613). Geneva, WHO.

2. Freud, A. (1966). Normality and Pathology in Childhood. London, Hogarth Press.

3. Department of Health and Social Security (1976). Fit for the Future: Report of the Committee on child health services. (Chmn Professor S D M Court) (Cmnd. 6684). London, HMSO.

4. General Register Office Scotland (1980) Mid-year population estimates. Edinburgh, GRO.

5. General Register Office Scotland (1979) Register General Scotland's Annual Report. Edinburgh, HMSO.

6. Richman, N. Stevenson, J. and Graham, P. (1975). Journal of Child Psychology and Psychiatry, *16*, 282.

7. Rutter, M. and Madge, N. (1976). Cycles of disadvantage. London, Heinemann.

8. Rutter, M. (1975). British Journal of Psychiatry, *126*, 493.

9. Rutter, M. Tizard, J. and Whitmore K, *eds* (1970). Education, Health and Behaviour. London, Longman.

10. Wedge, P. and Prosser, H. (1973). Born to Fail? London, Arrow Books in association with the National Children's Bureau.

11. Pringle, M. K. (1974). The Needs of Children: a Personal Perspective Prepared for the Department of Health and Social Security. London, Hutchison for National Children's Bureau.

12. Scottish Home and Health Department and Scottish Education Department (1980). Vulnerable Families: a Report by the Child Health Programme Planning Group of the Scottish Health Service Planning Council (Chmn. Dr A L Speirs). Edinburgh, HMSO.

13. Sheldon, E. (1972). The Sitter Service for the Handicapped, Aberdeen. Unpublished. Copies may be obtained from the Scottish Health Service Planning Council Secretariat, Room 205, St Andrew's House, Edinburgh.

14. Scottish Education Department (1974). Health Education in Schools. (Curriculum paper No. 14.) London, HMSO.

15. Baum, D. McFarlane, A. and Tizard, P. *in* Chard, T. and Richards, M. *eds.* (1977). Benefits and Hazards of the New Obstetrics. London, Spastics International Medical Publications.

16. Scottish Home and Health Department and Scottish Education Department (1979). A Better Life: Report on Services for the Mentally Handicapped in Scotland. A Report by a

Programme Planning Group of the Scottish Health Service Planning Council and the Advisory Council on Social Work. Edinburgh, HMSO.

17. Scottish Home and Health Department and Scottish Education Department (1980). Towards Better Health Care for School Children in Scotland: a Report by the Child Health Programme Planning Group of the Scottish Health Service Planning Council. Edinburgh, HMSO.

18. Scottish Education Department. Social Work Services Group (1981) Children in Care or under Supervision, Scotland, 1980 (Statistical bulletin) Edinburgh, the Department.

19. Jackson, B. and Jackson, S. (1979). Childminder: a Study in Action Research. London, Routledge and Kegan Paul.

20. Department of Education and Science, Scottish Office and Welsh Office (1978). Special Educational Needs. Report of the Committee of Enquiry into the Education of Handicapped Children and Young People. (Chmn Mrs H M Warnock). (Cmnd 7212). London, HMSO.

21. Scottish Education Department (1977). Truancy and Indiscipline in Schools in Scotland: (Chmn Professor D C Pack) Edinburgh, HMSO.

22. Committee of Scottish Local Authorities. Discipline in Scottish schools: Final Report of the Working Group on Corporal Punishment. Edinburgh, COSLA.

23. Education (Scotland) Acts 1980 and 1981.

24. Scottish Education Department (1978). The Education of Pupils with Learning Difficulties in Primary and Secondary Schools in Scotland: a Progress Report by HM Inspectors of Schools. Edinburgh, HMSO.

25. The Education of Handicapped Children and Young People (Chmn Mrs H M Warnock) (Cmnd 7212) London, HMSO.

26. Home Office (1968). Children in Trouble. (Cmnd 3601) London, HMSO.

27. Scottish Education Department, Social Work Services Group (1979). Intermediate Treatment in Scotland. Edinburgh, the Department.

28. Bruce, N. (1980). Teamwork for Preventive Care. London. Wiley.

29. Scottish Home and Health Department. Scottish Health Services Council (1970). The Staffing of Mental Deficiency Hospitals: Report of a Sub-Committee. (Chmn Sir I C R Batchelor). Edinburgh, HMSO.

30. House of Commons Select Committee (1977). Select Committee on Violence in the Family. First report, Session 1976-1977. Violence to children. London, HMSO.

31. Martin, F. M. Murray, K. and Fox, S. J. (1981). Children Out of Court. Edinburgh, Scottish Academic Press.

32. MIND (1975). Assessment of Children and their Families; Report produced by MIND Working Party. London, MIND and King's Fund Centre.

33. Scottish Education Department, Social Work Services Group (1971). Assessment of Children.

34. Holman, R. (1973). Trading in Children: a Study of Private Fostering. London, Routledge and Kegan Paul.

35. Wolfkind, S. (1978). Journal of Child Psychology, *19*, 393.

36. Department of Health and Social Security, Scottish Education Department and Welsh Office (1976). Guide to Fostering Practice. London, HMSO. (Cover title: Foster care: a guide to practice).

37. Central Council for Education and Training in Social Work (1973). Training for Residential Work. (CCETSW Discussion Document) London, the Council.

38. Central Council for Education and Training in Social Work (1974). Residential Work is Part of Social Work (CCETSW Paper 3) London, the Council.

39. Brunel Institute of Organisation and Social Studies (1974). Social Services Departments. London, Heinemann.

40. Residential Care Association (1979). The Social Work Task: an Introduction to the Analysis of the Social Work Task in Residential and Day Care Settings. London, Residential Care Association.

41. Personal Social Services Council (1975). Living and Working in Residential Homes. London, the Council.

42. Scottish Education Department. Social Work Services Group (1980). Social Work Case Statistics, 1979 (Statistical Bulletin). Edinburgh, the Department.

43. National Council of Social Service (1967). Caring for People: Staffing Residential Homes. (National Institute for Social Work Training Series No. 11) London, Allen and Unwin.

44. Rowe, J. and Lambert, L. (1973). Children who Wait: a Study of Children needing Substitute Families. Association of British Adoption and Fostering Agencies.

45. Scottish Education Department, Personal Communication.

46. Scottish Education Department, Social Works Services Group. Personal Communication.

47. Scottish Education Department (1974) Educational Staffing Ratios in List D Schools: Report of a Working Party. Edinburgh, the Department.

48. Cawson, P. and Martell, M. (1979). Children Referred to Closed Units. (DHSS Research Report No 5). London, HMSO.

49. Milham, S. et al (1981). Issues of Control in Residential Child Care. Department of Health and Social Security. London, HMSO.

50. Robins, L. (1966). Deviant Children Grown Up. Baltimore, Williams and Wilkins.

51. Scottish Education Department. Social Work Services Group. Medical and Social Work Interface. Edinburgh, the Department.

52. British Journal of Psychiatry. December (1973). News and Notes.

53. Scottish Home and Health Department (1973). Towards an Integrated Child Health Service. (Chmn Sir J Brotherston). Edinburgh, HMSO.

54. Royal Commission on the National Health Service (1979) Report. (Chmn Sir Alex Merrison) London, HMSO.

55. Child Guidance in the Eighties. (1981) Report of the Scottish Principal Educational Psychologists, Edinburgh.

56. Brown, S. Colvin, I. Scott, S. and Twiddle, E. *in* Barker, P. (1974). The Residential Psychiatric Treatment of Children. London, Crosby Lockwood.

57. Psychologists Associations Co-ordinating Team (1979). The Training of Educational Psychologists in Scotland: Report to Scottish Education Department. London, PACT.

58. Department of Health and Social Security (1980): Two Reports on Research into Services for Children and Adolescents. London, HMSO.

ADDITIONAL READING

British Medical Journal (1981). Hazards of Unemployment. British Medical Journal, *282*, 1179.

Department of Health for Scotland (1952). Child Health. Report of the Committee on Child Health of the Scottish Health Services Council. (Chmn. A Cunningham). Edinburgh, HMSO.

Department of Health and Social Security (1974). Report of the Committee on One-parent Families. (Chmn. Hon Sir Morris Finer). (Cmnd 5629). London, HMSO.

Department of Health and Social Security (1976). Manpower and Training for the Social Services. London, HMSO.

Department of Health and Social Security, Scottish Office and Welsh Office (1978). Special Educational Needs. London, HMSO.

Department of Education and Science (1967). Children and their Primary Schools. A Report of the Central Advisory Council for Education (England). London, HMSO.

Home Office (1968). Report of the Committee on Local Authority and Allied Personal Social Services. (Cmnd 3703) London, HMSO.

Home Office and Scottish Education Department (1972). Report of the Departmental Committee on the Adoption of Children. (Cmnd 5107). London, HMSO.

Martin, F. M. Fox, S. J. and Murray, K. (1981). Edinburgh, Scottish Academic Press.

Needs and Expectation in Obstetrics (1980). Health Bulletin (Edinburgh), *38*, 99.

Office of Population Censuses and Surveys (1976). Child Health: a Collection of Studies. (Studies on Medical and Population Subjects No. 31). London, HMSO.

Rogers,R. (1980). Crowther to Warnock (How Fourteen Reports Tried to Change Children's Lives). Heineman.

Royal Commission on the National Health Service (1979). Report (Chmn Sir Alex Merrison). (Cmnd 7615). London, HMSO.

Scottish Education Department, Social Work Services Group (1971). Assessment of children: Report of a Study Group. Edinburgh, the Department.

Scottish Education Department. Social Work Services Group (1979) Staff of Scottish Social Work Departments, 1978 (Statistical Bulletin). Edinburgh, the Department.

Scottish Education Department. Social Work Services Group (1980). Children's Hearings Statistics, 1979. (Statistical Bulletin). Edinburgh, the Department.

Scottish Education Department. Social Work Services Group (1981). Home Care Services, Day Care Establishments, Day Services, Scotland 1980. (Statistical bulletin). Edinburgh, the Department.

Scottish Education Department. Social Work Services Group. (1981). Residential Accommodation for Children, 1980. (Statistical Bulletin). Edinburgh, the Department.

Scottish Education Department. Social Work Services Group (1980). Staff of Scottish Social Work Departments. (Statistical Bulletin). Edinburgh, the Department.

Scottish Home and Health Department (1974). The Child Health Services. Edinburgh, the Department.

Scottish Home and Health Department and Scottish Education Department (1964). Children and Young Persons, Scotland. (Chmn. Lord Kilbrandon). (Cmnd 2306). Edinburgh, HMSO.

Special Educational Treatment (Scotland) Regulations 1954 (SI 1954) No. 1239.

World Health Organisation (1965) Child Health and the School. Geneva, WHO.

World Health Organisation (1969). Child Health; Report on a European Symposium. (EURO 1682) Geneva, WHO.

World Health Organisation (1976). New Trends and Approaches in the Delivery of Maternal and Child Care in Health Services. (Technical Report series No 600). Geneva, WHO.

CHILD AND ADOLESCENT MENTAL HEALTH WORKING GROUP

Chairman

Professor
Elisabeth Mapstone — Professor of Social Administration and Social Work, University of Dundee

Members

Miss B E Acton — Nursing Officer, Royal Hospital for Sick Children, Edinburgh

Dr I C Buchan — General Practitioner, Howden Health Centre, Livingston

Mr J Canizares — Nursing Officer, Young People's Unit, Royal Edinburgh Hospital

Mr D Davies — Headmaster, Ballikinrain School, Balfron, Glasgow

Dr J Evans — Consultant Psychiatrist, Young People's Unit, Royal Edinburgh Hospital

Dr A R Forrest — Principal Psychologist, List D Schools, Edinburgh

Miss L Kerr — Principal Educational Psychologist, Glasgow Division, Strathclyde Regional Council

Miss C McCall — Nursing Officer, Royal Hospital for Sick Children, Glasgow

Dr Valerie Marrian — Consultant Paediatrician, Royal Infirmary, Perth

Miss S Massey — Assistant Divisional Director (Residential), Barnardo's, Edinburgh

Dr I Menzies — Consultant Psychiatrist, Ninewells Hospital, Dundee

Dr H G Morton — Consultant Psychiatrist, Ninewells Hospital, Dundee

Mr J Rae	Assistant Director (Fieldwork), Borders Regional Council Social Work Department
Dr J Sharp	Principal Psychologist, Royal Hospital for Sick Children, Glasgow
Miss E Sheldon	Formerly Social Work Manager, Health Care Services, Grampian Regional Council
Mr A Sinclair	Reporter to Children's Panel, Borders Regional Council
Mr C Toppin	Headmaster, St Augustine's Secondary School, Glasgow

Assessors

Dr P W Brooks	Senior Medical Officer, Scottish Home and Health Department
Dr A T B Moir	Principal Medical Officer, Chief Scientist Organisation, Scottish Home and Health Department
Mr J I Smith	Senior Adviser, Social Work Services Group, Scottish Education Department

Secretariat

Mr T D Hunter
Mr P S Taylor until October 1981
Mrs F M Cruickshanks from February 1982

Printed in Scotland for HMSO. Dd. 0735739 C30 11/83